A GIRL'S GUIDE TO

growing Up

making the right choices

BY JUDITH E. GREENBERG

Franklin Watts
A Division of Grolier Publishing
New York   London   Hong Kong   Sydney
Danbury, Connecticut

To my son, Mitch,
  who has the talent and heart to inspire me, and
to my daughter, Wendi,
  who has the creativity and insight to astound me,
and in memory of my father
  who always supported my choices.

J.E.G.

Photographs ©: International Stock Photo: 8, 108 (Scott Barrow); Liaison Agency, Inc.: cover (Churchill & Klehr), 99 (Lara Jo Regan), 110 (Brian Smith); Photo Researchers: 17 (Damien Lovegrove/SPL), 90 (Ed Young/SPL); PhotoEdit: 129 (Robert Brenner), 50, 95 (Mary Kate Denny), 71 (Myrleen Ferguson), 35 (Tony Freeman), 19 (Will Hart), 39, 103 (Richard Hutchings), 116 (Tom McCarthy), 21, 45, 65, 123, 126 (Michael Newman), 10, 28, 48, 57, 81, 85, 106 (David Young-Wolff); Stock Boston: 42 (Daemmrich), 113 (Vincent DeWitt), 120 (Najlah Feanny), 25 (Grantpix), 62 (Gale Zucker); Tony Stone Images: 32 (Zigy Kaluzny), 53 (Ian O'Leary), 77 (Rosanne Olson), 29 (David Young-Wolff).

Visit Franklin Watts on the Internet at:
http://publishing.grolier.com

Library of Congress Cataloging-in-Publication Data

Greenberg, Judith E.
    A Guirl's Guide to Growing Up: Making the Right Choices/by Judith E. Greenberg
        p. cm.
    Includes bibliographical references and index.
    Summary: Discusses the issues faced by middle-school girls as they grow up, including personal relationships, school responsibilities, personal style and self-image, temptations, risky behavior, and the many decisions they must make.
    ISBN 0-531-11592-5 (lib.bdg.)   0-531-16542-6 (pbk.)
    1.Girls—United States—Social conditions—Juvenile literature. 2.Teenage girls—United States—Social conditions—Juvenile literature. 3. Young women—United States—Juvenile literature. 4. Choice (Psychology)—Juvenile literature. [1. Teenage girls. 2. Conduct of life] I. Title.

HQ798.G69 2000
305.23—dc21   99-088229

GROLIER
PUBLISHING

©2000 by Judith E. Greenberg
All rights reserved. Published simultaneously in Canada.
Printed in the United States of America
1 2 3 4 5 6 7 8 9 10 R 09 08 07 06 05 04 03 02 01 00

Acknowledgments

A SPECIAL THANK-YOU to Sarah Troxel, who shared her feelings and poetry in this book. The poem "I Came to Myself" was written by Laura Slater and is published here with permission from the West Nottingham Academy Literary Advance, Spring 1999. A third poet, Dawn Bresnahan, is thanked for her poem "Tooth Fairy."

From the author's mind to the bookshelf, many people help to make a book a reality: Super thanks to Dalia Amir and Michelle Lobos for their outstanding research, constant support, and generous supply of strawberry milkshakes. Thank you to Larissa Kushnir, a young woman who has just grown past the age this book was written for, and who gave the manuscript a good, critical reading. A debt of gratitude is owed to my editor, Lorna Greenberg, who always makes my books seem special and continues to be patient.

Finally, I wish to give my appreciation to the many women professionals who gave of their time and expertise to help young teens learn about making good choices.

Contents

1

Understanding Growing Up Female

YELLOW BRICK ROAD

Life's a never-ending road
Full of twists and turns
Double backs
And cloverleaves.
Pick a path
And follow it through
Left or right
Which way to go?
Straight ahead
Follow the North Star
Find your way in the dark.
Follow a trail of crumbs,
Walk along
Traffic rushing by
Seems like you're
Going so slowly
Left behind
All those flying by.
Five years down the road
Will you be stuck on the shoulder?
Put on your shoes
And follow the yellow brick road home.
Get stuck in a field of poppies
And never reach your
Emerald City.
Put on your blinders
And trudge through.
Life's a never-ending road
Full of twists and turns
Double backs
And cloverleaves.

HAVE YOU EVER felt that there was another you inside yourself? One who was prettier, smarter, luckier, healthier, and richer. One who knew what she wanted to do. Do you wish that "other you" would get out and throw away the you that has a different learning style, a big shoe size, doesn't know how to talk to boys, and often feels unable to fit in at school or home? Although this may sound like a bad script for a daytime talk show, many girls in middle school and early high school do not feel very good about themselves. Some girls might talk with a friend about their problems and feelings, or ask for help from a father or a mother. Brothers and sisters, especially if they are older and have experienced the same feelings, are also helpful. Then again, some girls might hold their pain very deeply inside until it gets sore and sickly and colors all their emotions.

Growing up presents many choices.

This book is designed to help you understand many of the issues that young women face today. If you are between ten and fifteen years old, you might find help, information, and encouragement by reading this book. The focus of the book is important, and needs to be emphasized as much as possible: Many choices will be presented to you as you grow up. With information and alternatives to consider, you can make wise and safe choices.

Before making a choice, before acting on a decision, consider the responsible choices and the consequences. Also be sure to remember that you are never really alone; there is always somewhere to turn and someone who will help you. Many teachers will help students through rough times or just be there to listen. Relatives can always be called upon. And a male point of view is often helpful, especially if you want to understand why a boy has acted a certain way.

Each chapter looks at specific choices that girls must make and provides information and guidance from other girls and advice from female professionals. There are many professional women, such as psychiatrists, psychologists, counselors, and family doctors, who spend their working time helping young women to mature into healthy adults. The "To Find Out More" section at the end of this book lists many resources and hotlines if you want or need more help. You have made your first choice by beginning to read this book. As the author, I want to welcome you and remind you that you don't have to face this stage of your life alone.

Many facets of life are hard for girls in the ten- to fifteen-year-old category to get used to but they need to become part of your learning experience. The teen years have never been considered easy. Adolescents vary widely during their years of growing into adulthood. Between ages eleven through eighteen, you will begin to menstruate, which, as your hormones change monthly, may cause mood swings, depression, and negative feelings. Many girls grow tall and develop feminine bodies, while their friends still look like young girls. Weighing just the right amount can be overemphasized during adolescence and may cause undue stress or a shaky ego.

Confusion about your social role can make family events and teenage parties tough to manage. Two questions that bother girls are "Where do I fit in?" and "Who are my real friends?" Just as toddlers like to test out their new mobility, teens become curious about their new bodies, attitudes, and seesawing emotions. This is also a time when girls will look for a chance to argue with parents and family members and quibble over the slightest details. The confusion you feel can be as difficult as getting adjusted to your new body and responsibilities. The good news is that although life may seem negative, adolescence doesn't last long, and you can make life better by concentrating on goals that you can accomplish.

As the author, I have tried to look at sad, scary, and dangerous topics so that you can become better informed and better able to make intelligent, safe choices. Each chapter allows you the opportunity to peek into situations in which girls have had to face difficult things. Some situations may sound like something that has happened to you or your best friend or the girl who sits behind you in English class. You have an opportunity to learn consequences through the mistakes or good choices of girls mentioned in the book.

> **SITUATION**
> Should you take the short cut home?
>
> **GOOD CHOICE**
> Take the well lit, busy street.

Sometimes choices are not too difficult to make and might not have a big effect on your everyday life. If you make the girls' middle-school basketball team, you would need to organize your schedule. You'll want to make it to classes and to practice, to get your homework done and your chores completed, and to still have time for friends. Unless you make choices about how to spend your time each day, you can't fit in everything you want or need to do. This time shortage will require that you make priorities and decide which responsibility must come first and which can be done later or on another day. Obviously, this type of choice is not as difficult as deciding whether to smoke or drink. However, every choice you face requires conscious choice-making.

Sometimes choices are forced on us by peer pressure. Reading this book may help you to see that many alternatives exist in each situation. There is always somewhere to turn, and this book will give you suggestions. The most important thing to remember is that no crisis lasts a lifetime and that there is always someone to help you through it. Never give up—there is help available that is free and given by people who want to keep you safe. When girls have logical and realistic choices at their fingertips, life is much brighter, safer, and more fun. As you read this book, keep in mind that no one is preaching at you or trying to make you feel young and foolish. If a situation makes you feel that you are in jeopardy, you need to be prepared to face it and make the safest decision.

The writer of most of the poems in this book is a girl not much older than you. Sarah is an exotic-looking young woman with great intelligence, good grades, and a super relationship with her family. She wrote these poems a few years ago, at a different time in her life. Her concerns and adolescent pain come through strongly in each poem. Look for your own feelings in the poetry and think of how the poet found her way from this anguish to be happy today. Sarah hopes that knowing how sad she felt and how inadequate she thought she was will help you to realize someone else felt this way. Discussing her feelings with her family and a professional helped her overcome most of her problems.

When you are finished with this book, give it to a friend. Your parents might want to look at it too. Then someone who loves and understands you will be ready to help you and to admire your responsible choices as you grow into a strong adult female.

School, Home, and Street Choices

2

WATERS

I dream of waters
I've never seen
I dream of a home
I've never known
I'm drawn to water
Bluer than the sky.
When the sun shines
I hear the sea
Calling me home
When the wind blows
I hear waves whispering
To me and I know
That where the sky
Meets the sea
She'll be waiting
For me to come home
To the water that
Calls me daughter.

TINA IS THIRTEEN years old and looking forward to her next school break. Tina hates school because it takes her longer than most of her classmates to find the answers inside her head. Sometimes she answers incorrectly, and her teacher makes her feel pretty stupid. Then, at lunch, all the other kids tease her about the wrong answer, and she feels worse. By the time Tina goes home for the day, she has a lot of homework and catch-up work as well. She also has chores; tonight she has to set the table and clean her room. Tina's mom wants her to be more responsible, and her dad says that she is lazy and needs to work harder and keep her mouth closed at school. It hasn't been a good day for Tina and it is typical of how most days make her feel.

Tina goes to her room after dinner to start her work and is often sound asleep before she gets through the math problems. The next day, Tina is afraid to go to school unprepared, so she decides to skip school.

Does Tina sound like someone you know? Many students in schools all over the country have bad days because they learn differently from the other students. In Tina's case, she has ADHD, attention deficit hyperactivity disorder. She is quite bright, but sometimes it takes longer for her to understand directions, she never seems to have enough time to finish tests, and she has trouble paying attention to her teachers. It seems as if she is trying to find the answers but they are lost inside her brain, and when she does remember, it is too late. Some days Tina is confused about how to start an assignment and tries to get to the teacher's desk to ask for an explanation. By the time Tina gets through the nearly thirty other students asking the teacher questions, it is time to

Arguments with parents may erupt over minor details.

get to her next class, or her teacher has to get ready to teach the next students. Many days, Tina takes her homework home, intending to do it, only to find out she really doesn't understand the assignment. Then she just gives up on it. Sometimes she gets part of the way through the assignment but forgets to turn it in the next day, or decides it isn't finished and that the teacher will turn it down. Tina is afraid to take chances in her work because she has failed so many times. Her self-esteem is low, and she doesn't want to make any more mistakes.

Many students have a different style of learning from that of the majority of students: Some students do better when they see visual examples of the information being taught, others need to hear rather than read the information, and still others learn best by acting out information. Learning differently can make school hard and often boring, but with teachers who try to teach Tina in a style that helps her understand, she can get higher grades with less frustration. Sometimes students with ADHD do better in smaller classes, tutors can help, and sometimes a doctor might recommend medicine or a special diet to help the students be more alert during school hours.

What Do the Experts Say?

Dr. Laura Thompson has researched, written, and given lectures on the topic of food and brain function. She suggests that parents find out more about the connection between nutrition and the way the brain works, as there have been "many discoveries about the important role of nutrition in health and how it affects the

Work with your teachers to discover the best way for you to learn.

mental and emotional states of children." Students who eat foods with a lot of sugar often have trouble paying attention in class. Fresh vegetables, fruits, and proteins help a student be more receptive to what is being taught.

Another expert, an educational consultant who helps children find schools that are better suited to their learning styles, offers some important advice. If school is difficult for you, make a list of the classes you like, and describe how each of those teachers run the classroom. Is the class all lecture, all textbook, or very visual? Do you get to make things and do projects? Discover how you learn the best. Then, try to use those learning strengths in every class. Let your teachers in on what you've learned.

Also, don't let your attitude get you into trouble at school. Teachers want to respect their students. Acting like a stuck-up movie-star-wanna-be makes a teacher think you are not interested in learning. Then you start to feel that the teacher dislikes you, and it is hard to do your best work. Soon your grades drop. Treat teachers and other students with respect, and you will be treated the way you enjoy.

It takes courage to go to school every day when being there feels uncomfortable. But if you are feeling bad or hurt in class, keep in mind that you are not the only one. Many students who are labeled "different" find school a nightmare of dark halls, shouting teachers, and too many other students. If you feel out of place at school, chances are you have low self-esteem. The phrase *self-esteem* is used frequently by educators and health professionals. It simply means self-confidence combined with self-respect. Believing in yourself is an important component of self-esteem and success at school.

If you are truly unable to feel competent or if you are getting ill from stress (pressures of keeping up grades, sitting still in class, or the prospect of a failing performance), you should talk to your parents about these feelings. This is a situation where you have a choice. In your attempt to make yourself feel better, you may turn to drinking or drugs or just give up on school. Or you can resolve to ask for help, keep working, and think about your strengths. Making a choice is not always easy. Sometimes the hard choice hurts now but will be better in the long run. But as with many other situations, choosing to talk to someone is the only way to be understood and to get help for these troubling feelings and behaviors.

A caring parent can help you understand your feelings.

How to Seek Help at School

You or your parents can ask for a meeting with your teachers and counselor to discuss why classes are hard for you and what the teachers might do that would help you. For example, if you have ADHD or other learning differences, many school systems are ready to help you with some accommodations. You might be provided with a tutor, or someone to take notes for you, or a laptop to use in class. You may be allowed extended time for tests, or the right to ask the teacher to explain directions on a test.

Many ADHD students do not understand their problem very well. They don't want to talk to their parents or teachers about it, but the problem grows each marking period and then each year. Parents get worried and wonder why their child is unhappy and tired and hates school. It takes a strong person to make the choice to say, "I hate school. It's hard, the teachers don't like me, and I can't learn like the other kids." It takes courage to share your worries and fears. Choosing to be mature about a problem is the best way to start understanding your learning style. Whether you have ADHD, are dyslexic (reverse letters and numbers), or have trouble processing information, knowledge always helps, since it is what we don't know about ourselves that scares us the most.

There are many people who can help you and your parents. Your family doctor is a good place to start. Other people with the ability to help include a nutritionist, a specialist who may test you and help your family decide if medication is appropriate, school counselors and psychologists, and the teachers and school principal.

More Ways to Work with Your Parents

Once you have started talking with your parents, try talking about other things that are important to you now. Your music tastes are probably different from those of your parents. Some of the songs your parents listen to may make you laugh, and they may not want you playing your music at home. Choices again! What should you do? This is an easy one: Just keep your music low, or use headphones. Learning to make wise choices is a bit like learning to play a sport. You need to develop your talent and skills and also learn the strategy to make the right moves.

Having a good strategy saves a lot of time that might be wasted in arguing. Many parents are very strict, and you are probably just beginning to push against rules that have been in place since childhood. Especially if both your parents work, or yours is a one-parent home, the rules may be fairly rigid. Parents often do not realize when a teen is ready to venture out.

Spending time at a movie and the mall may sound good to you but dangerous to your protectors, your parents. Perhaps they have read about girl groups shoplifting at the mall, or boys who follow groups of girls making obscene gestures and noises. In many cases, parents want to keep you away from situations that offer only difficult choices, and until they see that you make mature and responsible decisions, don't expect them to back down. Keeping you safe has been a major job for them for a long time, and they often worry about unfamiliar things. Your choices are to lie and go anyway, to yell at them about how mean they are, or to accept that you need to do some more work on your own actions.

Prove that you can take care of yourself by being responsible. When you cheat on your folks, you may get away with it, but you may also get caught big time! Remember, it's a choice you make. Make it a good one so your parents' fears can subside.

No one likes being scared, but teens need to be aware that the outside world can be unsafe. Teens often feel that their parents are being silly and imagining dangers. Saying "Everything is cool" doesn't work because your parents are not making up the things that can happen. Some people drink and then drive. Some people steal. Not everything is cool. You could be in the path of the car or the thief's gun. Television and movies make the world seem like a wild place with some very exciting things to do, but they often neglect to show the consequences.

Being street smart, knowing which places are dangerous and which are not, is the best way to keep yourself safe. There are many things you could do to be safe going to and from school or a friend's house. Carry a small flashlight, or have a pager so that your parents can be in touch with you. (Remember, pagers are usually not allowed in school.) Having a pager makes it possible for your parents to know where you are, in case you need a ride or don't call home at the right time. A pager also lets you get in touch with your parents.

Travel in groups so that you can't be lost or left alone if hurt. And remember the grade school instructions: Don't take candy from a stranger, don't get in a stranger's car. Tell someone where you are going. Young people tend to believe they will be safe, even if the situation is not. Sometimes you'll see friends rush straight

*Time together, without pressure, gives you a chance to become friends
with your parents.*

into danger, as if they believe they are bulletproof. This is a defen-
sive action that covers up actual fears. Unfortunately, it can moti-
vate reckless and dangerous choices. There are situations that a
teen, or an adult, cannot handle, and there are dangerous places.
We all need to be street smart and make smart choices.

Schools Can Be Unsafe

Dangerous situations can occur in schools too—even though that's a place that should be safe. We've read reports of a popular teacher being accused of being a pedophile (an adult who prefers children as sex partners). In an East Coast town, a drama teacher was accused of coaxing girls as young as fourteen to be photographed in sexy poses wearing skimpy clothes. He then put the photos on the Internet. Most of the girls' parents did not let their daughters come forward as witnesses and even refused to let the police talk to them. Only one girl was able to make the choice to be a witness; the police withheld her identity.

The teacher had talked this girl into having a sexual relationship. Had she been more street smart and perhaps more sure of her own worth, she might not have been so easily persuaded. But was it a poor choice or a lack of a choice? Did she realize she had a choice?

In many middle schools across the country, some students hide knives in their clothing just in case they need protection. Some school bathrooms may be taken over by gang members, to hang out. They are therefore off limits to everyone else. Students copy those who have made bomb threats or actual bombs as a way of looking important. Of course, these dangerous behaviors lead to expulsion and sometimes criminal charges when the students are found out. Schools in small towns and big cities have at times become places of possible danger, when unhappy students try to get atten-

> **SITUATION**
> A stranger comes up to talk.
>
> **GOOD CHOICE**
> If the conversation seems O.K. (ex. asking for directions), answer briefly and walk away. Otherwise, just walk away.

tion or deal with their unhappiness or fear with inappropriate behavioral choices.

Sometimes girls fear that if they stay home from a party or leave early to go home, they will be teased or accused of acting "childish." If you feel that you are in a situation that will get out of hand or already is, think through your priorities and make a choice. Good friends will support your choice and go with you; the others may be people you choose not to have as friends anymore.

Conflicts at school can be fairly common events for many young girls. Sometimes students may try to insult you, just to see if they can make you angry. Older students might start an argument to make you look immature; you might even get hit by another student just because you looked at her in a "funny" way. Learning that you don't have to respond will help you to better deal with insults. Instead of responding, get a grip on your own feelings of anger. We all need to accept responsibility for our own anger. You may become angry, but no one besides you can make you act angry.

Once you know what has made you angry, look at what caused the other person to be angry. Was there a misunderstanding you can straighten out? Avoid saying words that have emotional triggers such as, "I hate you" or "I'm going to kill you." If a person seems out of control, try to keep your cool and wait for him or her to cool down. Count to ten, or walk away.

Sometimes a girl can feel that her friends are criticizing her or talking about her behind her back. But criticism and disapproval are not the same. Criticism hurts, but a friend may be letting you know that too much makeup makes your eyes look sad instead of

Criticism may hurt, but it can be a friend's way of trying to help you.

pretty. Perhaps there is something worth learning from a situation like this. A good friend may offer criticism meant to help you, but disapproval is being told that what you do can't be accepted by the crowd, so get lost. The difference is great. The friend is trying to help; the others are being mean.

How you deal with these conflicts and communication glitches shows your maturity and responsibility. By accepting well-meaning criticism, you may be building a support system of friends who

Some good activity helps work out anger and stress.

feel they can be honest with you and expect the same in return. All teens, girls and boys, benefit from a strong support system. These are the people who love you and care about your well-being—including parents, other relatives, friends, and teachers.

You may also wish to learn more about how to relax so that unkind words and actions do not hurt or lead you to strike out in response. Use deep breathing, yoga, a mantra, or an outlet such as shooting baskets to relieve and master the angers, fears, or tensions that may have built up during a hard day at school, a game, or at a friend's house.

Rejection at school hurts, but there are things you can do. Knowing that a boy's rejection probably means he is scared silly by girls helps. When girlfriends leave you out, you can choose to find other friends who are more open to being friendly.

School, home, and the streets you travel need to be safe for you to grow and be happy. The choices you make and the way you act can have a great deal to do with your happiness and success.

Tempting, Isn't It? 3

NOT MINE

Did you think maybe I forgot?
Oh no.
I remembered every word you said
And now I've come for revenge.
After years of being afraid and alone
I finally realized
That you're the one holding me back.
And all I gotta do
Is get rid of you.
Did you think maybe I forgot?
Oh no.
I remember everything you did,
And now I've come for revenge.
After years of being afraid and alone
I finally realized
That I didn't do anything wrong.
All the shame is yours,
Not mine.
None of it is mine
It's yours, not mine.

AFTER SPENDING FIVE days at a rehabilitation center for teenage alcohol and drug abusers, I realized that teens who do not believe that they are harming themselves or that they have a habit are not ready to be in recovery. The first step toward recovery is taking your head out of the sand and admitting that you have a problem. Teens need to take responsibility for their actions and their choice of friends. Choosing friends who drink and drive or who abuse drugs can put you in a very difficult situation. If you are caught with these friends, you will be treated as they are and could be arrested along with them. You might even end up in juvenile court.

A group therapy session at a teen rehab center

While at the rehab center, I learned many facts about the diseases of alcoholism and drug abuse. An alcoholic is a person who drinks regularly to get to a level of just feeling normal. Some alcoholics drink so much at parties that they forget what they did. Alcoholism and addiction are diseases, and they are chronic—they don't go away. Alcoholism and addiction are progressive—they get worse as time goes on, and they can be fatal. Your liver or other organs may give out, making you extremely ill. Continuing to drink or take drugs is a compulsive behavior, one that is dreadfully hard to control. This means the alcoholic will do anything to get a drink, and the addict will do anything to get drugs. An alcoholic is driven to drink and the addict is driven to drugs because they depend on their daily amount just to keep feeling normal—not high, but regular.

You are not a bad person if you have these diseases, but the diseases are definitely bad. Alcoholism and drug addiction can be hereditary (a tendency is passed down from a prior generation), but not all children in a family will inherit it. Alcoholism can skip a generation to show up later. Like the color of your eyes or hair, alcoholism is often controlled by your genetic makeup.

What Does an Expert Say?

Donna Schecter, a rehabilitation counselor at the center I visited, wants teens to know that "alcoholism is a powerful, cunning, and baffling disease. This goes for marijuana, cocaine, and heroin abuse as well. The definition of addiction, used by most rehab counselors and therapists, is as follows: a compulsive behavior [an act you feel you must do], that a person continues to do in spite of the consequences to oneself and others." She adds that girls and young teens may feel stressed by home and school or be depressed about grades, friends, and life in general. Drinking or abusing drugs is an effort to self-medicate the pain that is often a part of a girl's life in the early teens.

Ms. Schecter reminds us that alcoholism has not always been considered a disease. In fact, if you read a book published before the mid-1950s, it probably will not say that alcoholism is a disease. However, in 1954, the American Medical Association determined that alcoholism is a disease. This decision opened the door for many drinkers to get help because they were sick, not criminals.

Look at your family, on your father's and mother's side. Learn about relatives as far back as great-grandparents. Did anyone have a drinking problem? If they did, then you might be at greater risk. Even if they did not, alcohol and drugs are dangerous. It is important to remember that you can become an alcoholic through repeated use, even if your family members are not. This means you must choose whether or not to drink at parties or at a friend's house.

Feeling anxious in a crowd of other teens, wanting to be accepted by an older group of friends, not feeling secure about yourself, or not knowing how to say no without being embarrassed, can all lead to accepting a beer. This is one of the hardest choices you will face as a teen. Girls often have to make this choice at a time when being part of the crowd and being grown-up is very important.

You have the choice to say no to a beer.

Schecter asks readers to try to imagine a day in the life of an alcoholic. To help your imagination, let's make you a surgeon at a hospital in Arizona. You have a husband and three children, and you have won awards for your use of new techniques in surgery. You are a generally happy woman and do not really notice how much you drink. Yet family members are starting to mumble about your drinking habit. How do you know if your family is right? There is a simple group of questions to ask yourself to determine if your drinking has gotten hold of your life. Do not lie, especially to yourself.

1. Did you ever have a total loss of memory about a drinking episode? This memory loss is known as a blackout. Your eyes are open and you participate, however, you have no memory of the event or what you did.
2. Do you gulp booze down to get enough before someone finds out? Are you sneaky about your drinking?
3. Do you lie to cover up your drinking activities?
4. Do you drink alone?
5. Are you becoming less interested in friends? Do you turn down activities if there won't be any drinking or choose some because there will be?
6. Have you had to go to a doctor or hospital because drinking made you ill?
7. Do you protect your supply by hiding it and then moving it around so that no one finds it?
8. Do you have fears that make no sense? Do you feel as if people are out to get you?
9. Do you resent nondrinkers and choose your friends from the drinking crowd? Do your friends encourage your drinking?
10. Do you ever shake and feel as if a drink could make you feel normal?

Any "yes" answers are signs of alcoholism.

You or your parents may think you don't need to read about alcoholism now. Schecter stresses that the reality is that by ninth grade a large number of girls have already tried beer and marijuana, and may be choosing to be with friends who drink or use drugs.

A Police Officer Wants You to Know a Few Facts

Officer Angela Lintel is a special police officer who works with middle-school and high-school students. Her job includes speaking to students to try to prevent them from starting to drink and use drugs. Officer Lintel reminds readers of some of the consequences of drug and alcohol use. Every state has an age limit for drinking; you must be twenty-one years old. The reason for this restriction is that most young people are not mature enough to handle drinking and drug use. Their bodies are insufficiently developed for such activities.

"Also there are very strict laws that judges must follow if a young person is arrested for drinking or drug use," says Officer Lintel. Judges are required to give long jail sentences if selling drugs is involved. You will have a police record, and this information can be passed along to employers, police officers, the community, and possibly even your family."

The officer also wants to be sure you understand that abusing household items such as glue or even whipped-cream cans to become high has been known to cause death. "Smoking cigarettes is also a high-risk and expensive habit. Cigarettes are fairly easy to obtain, and they have toxins that can harm you. Middle school is a time when students often, or want to, try smoking. You can become addicted very quickly and hardly realize that it is happening. The advertisements of tobacco companies make smoking look exciting. Ads and other students may try to convince you that you look more mature, interesting, or cool if you smoke. The end result is always the same: addiction, opening yourself to diseases such as cancer, and smelling like an old chimney! If you are offered anything to inject, smoke, drink, or inhale, be very careful. The substance can cause you to lose consciousness, suffer brain injury, or die from toxic combinations."

Once you reach middle school, teachers, parents, and friends will expect that you can make decisions; however, good decisions need information and education. If you want to learn more about the disease of alcoholism and how it affects the drinker and the family, you can call or go on the Internet for Al-Anon (for family members) or find meetings that are held in your community. Alateen is for teens who have a drinking family member. It is a place to safely talk to others who have a similar problem and learn about the many choices you have and the help that is available.

You Can Recover

To get well, an alcoholic or an addict needs a period of time away from the world to think and clear up a very fogged and confused brain. First the person's body has to get clear of the drink or the drug. Then the mind clears. Being sick, an alcoholic or addict needs to be committed to getting well. It is a long and hard road.

An addict may be dependent on alcohol, cigarettes, or a variety of substances.

The choice to get sober is not easy to make. It is harder than the choice to drink or take drugs.

People who work with alcoholics try to teach them to be responsible again. Alcoholics need courage to accept their feelings and work on their problems. Has one of your parents ever looked at your homework assignments and then noticed that you didn't bring home the right book or worksheet? You were probably told at that point that you must become more responsible. Yet how do you learn to be responsible, and who shows you?

The dictionary defines *responsibility* as a noun and includes phrases like "taking control of one's life," "being consistent about requirements," and "watching out for the welfare of yourself and others." When you are responsible, you are able to respond to what you feel. If it is anxiety or shame or fear, being responsible is setting out to find out why and then doing something about it. Alcoholics and other substance abusers must take responsibility for their habits. No matter what they smoke, drink, swallow, sniff, or inject, they are addicts. They react in a chemically induced way and are dependent on their abusive habit.

Many young teens forget about risks when experimenting and trying new thrills at parties. They forget that they may throw up in public, pass out, say or do stupid things, be hung over the next few days, or develop a taste for stronger thrills. The consequences of one night can last a lifetime. No one wins a scholarship by drinking. No one makes true friends by drinking. No one gets closer to her family by drinking. But everyone who drinks is an accident waiting to happen. If you drive drunk or get into a car with a drunk driver, you risk your life and the safety of your friends. If you need some stronger words to help you accept this fact, try to remember a seventeen-year-old girl driving drunk with three friends who crashed into a tree, killing her friends and beheading herself. People who drive drunk drivers risk long jail terms, expensive fines, and the loss of their license for a few years.

Are There Other Ways You May Be Hurt?

A Maryland county police publication lists some factors that increase a person's risks of becoming a victim. If you are drunk or high, you are more vulnerable to being attacked or raped. When you are not thinking clearly, it is easier to be the target or victim of a crime. Such trauma can scar you. It may sound preachy, but your best choice is to avoid drinking and drugging as if they were plagues and to say "no" for your own good. Female teen victims often know their attackers, are victimized near or at

> **SITUATION**
> You get a threatening or obscene phone call.
>
> **GOOD CHOICE**
> Hang up immediately. If repeated, or frightening, call police or the telephone company's annoyance call bureau.

school, and do not report the incident. These facts may help to explain why parents always want to know where you are going, who you are with, and how to reach you. These facts also give a good reason for a curfew. Your parents are trying to protect you from harm and victimization.

Professional Help Is Vital

Peggy McMann is a licensed clinical social worker and an alcohol and drug rehabilitation counselor who practices in Washington,

At Alateen or other peer group meetings, teens can get help in dealing with their own drinking, or that of a family member.

D.C. Ms. McMann says that she usually works with entire families, as it is not just the alcoholic who suffers—the whole family lives with the disease. She says that the kids who are in the least danger of getting into booze and drugs are "those whose parents are involved in parenting and in maintaining sobriety." A child who grows up in a codependent house (one where one or both parents drink and the spouse who may not drink doesn't object) is "more in danger of becoming an alcoholic because of the pain caused by living in a dysfunctional family. It is easy for a girl to drift toward a real gang or a group that is like a gang in that it sets rules and begins to be a substitute family." McMann ends by saying that "parents who are involved from the day of birth are more likely to have children who don't get pregnant at an early age and who don't become drinkers." If you worry about your drinking or that of a family member, McMann suggests you call 888-4AL-ANON, or e-mail: *wso@al-anon.alateen.org*. Someone will answer and help you, or a volunteer will call back. If you wonder if you, a friend, or a family member is an alcoholic, look at the Alcohol–Drug Use Questionnaire at the end of this book. McMann comments that "some questions do not apply to teens, but they do apply to your parents, and thus they are included in the test so that you may talk with a family member about your concern."

McMann is also concerned about other things girls may be doing to themselves. One area of concern is body tattooing and piercings.

As most body piercing is done without anesthesia, you are completely awake during the process. Have you seen the size of the needle that is pushed through your nose or your tongue? Body piercing dates back to ancient times. The Egyptians pierced their navels as a sign of royalty. Piercing and tattooing have become increasingly popular practices among American teens who follow fads. The most common areas for tattoos include shoulders, upper arms, and inside the wrists and ankles. Piercing is usually seen on earlobes, noses, tongues, navels, lips, and eyebrows.

When girls were asked why they tattoo or pierce, the answers were varied. Some said, "It's cool," "I like it," "It's a way to express myself," It's who I am," "My body is like a canvas," and "It's attractive."

Before you pierce or get tattooed, find out about the procedure and who is doing it. Ask friends for references, and then be sure the place is clean and that the needle to be used on you is in an unbroken, sterile package. Evaluate piercing stores or tattoo artists by asking if they heat-sterilize their instruments, how they dispose of the needles, and whether they wear sterile gloves for every new procedure. These questions are crucial since people who do piercing or tattooing can pass on hepatitis B or HIV.

You may know your reasons for piercing, but are you aware of the risks? For example, there is a risk of scarring and infection. Check all new piercings for several weeks for signs of infection, such as redness, pain, or tenderness. There might even be swelling and a discharge from the site of the piercing. Problems with nose piercing are similar to those with earlobe piercing. Tongues are high-risk areas because there are so many germs in the mouth. A girl can also lose her sense of taste or develop a numb tongue. The jewelry you choose is important in avoiding complications. Brass

How will you feel about that tattoo or piercing in ten years?

or nickel may cause allergic reactions. Surgical steel or 14K gold works best for most people.

Tattooing carries risks of infection, scarring, and being stuck with a label or a picture or symbol you really don't like. It is expensive and painful to get rid of tattoos.

Just as drinking and using drugs can be painful experiences, fads can be tempting, but also troublesome. Being responsible about your choices is essential. Living your whole life with the consequences of choices made when you were only a young teen might be difficult. Before you pierce or tattoo, think of what you will look like in five years or twenty years, and what you will tell your children when they want a matching rose on their ankles.

Date: It's Not Just a Four-Letter Word

TRUTH

Float
High above
In the air.
Look down on yourself.
Watch with an outside
Point of view.
Are you still thinking
The same way?
Step back
and
Watch
From the side.
Do you still
Feel the same?
Or can you see
the
Truth?

SANDRA WAS JUST about to leave for a party when her older brother yelled, "Mom, Dad, come see what Sandra is wearing." That's when her parents threw a fit about her tiny skirt. Sandra tried explaining that the outfit wasn't sexy; it was just cool. Her dad got angry and shouted at her, about giving out dangerous messages and that the skirt wasn't cool, but provocative. Sandra's mom ordered her to change into jeans or miss the party. Sandra did as she was told but still felt they were wrong and she was right.

Schoolwork, home responsibilities, and relaxing and spending time with friends are all important parts of teen life.

As Sandra's father was trying to say, rapists may select a particular female by how she looks. Rape, however, is an act of violence and wearing a paper sack will not protect you from an attack. On the other hand, your clothes could be sending a message that being sexy is all that matters to you, and boys may not take the time to learn what you care about because they are too busy looking at that tiny skirt! Your clothing might draw attention from males on the street or in school who shout nasty comments and suggestions at you. Answering them may lead them to say more or laugh at you. If people get used to seeing you dress that way, you'll keep getting the remarks even if you wear a skirt past your knees. This may turn some dates or parties into very upsetting evenings.

Dating and going to parties should be the relaxation and fun you earn after a hard week at school. But like everything else that you are growing into as a teen, dating is a serious venture. Once again the word *choices* comes into your life, and you will have many choices to make as you begin to date.

Alcoholism has already been discussed; however, two important points need to be mentioned in relation to dating and drinking. First, it is against the law for anyone to sell or give you alcohol. Second, alcohol can make you feel strange and act strange, or in ways you wouldn't normally act. There is a reason that you need to be twenty-one before buying drinks: Most people under the age of twenty-one do not handle alcohol with respect or good judgment. Actually, many people over the age of twenty-one do not do very well with alcohol either.

Continuing with the serious issues of dating, even if a female chooses to make out on a date, a boy does not have the right to expect further sex or intercourse. A girl may feel desire too, but she has a right to choose how far she wants to go. (So does a boy.) A female always has the right to say "no" at any point of a date or a party. No male has a right to push himself onto you or tell you that you are a tease or say that "you're asking for it." You control the situation. And, of course, no girl should talk a boy into a sexual encounter or push herself on an unwilling male. If your date continues to grope at you or tries to force you into a sexual situation that you do not wish to join, get away.

How do you physically overcome a strong young man? These suggestions apply to dates, people on public transportation, and

Schools and community centers offer training in self-defense and ways to protect against aggressive behavior.

anyone coming up to you in the street. You kick, grab, or twist any sensitive place on the male body. This includes kneecaps (kick hard), shins (kick or stomp with your heel), nose (take the heel of your hand and jam it up against the male's nose), penis (knee him or grab hold and twist hard). Any of these maneuvers should give you a head start to get away. Also, yell loudly and go to a friend, a friend's parent, a store owner, a cab driver, a police officer, or the house of someone you know near-by for help.

Never feel that you have caused this turn of events. You may have thought you wanted to partake of sex with a boyfriend, but you always have the right to decide not to, and if you say no, that's that. Don't be talked into anything you are not ready for or do not want to do, and do not feel guilty about it.

It may seem to you that all guys ever do is dream about sex, talk about sex, and spend their time trying to get some sex. Actually, you may be very close to the truth. One study found that males from ages twelve to nineteen think about sex nearly once every five minutes! Females of the same age group do not spend that much time involved in sexual dreams and desires. This is one rea-son guys misread signals; they want your smile to mean something more than you actually mean.

Apart from these more serious risks of dating, there are other topics to think about. Think about how you feel when a boy you like kisses you. As you mature both physically and emotionally, you will like kissing a special boy. It is normal to feel warm, to have your heartbeat increase, and even to want him to touch your body. If you do not have these physical feelings, you may not be ready yet to experience those kinds of feelings in general, or with this particular boy.

You may want to talk with your mother, an older sibling, or your dad about how to handle these new feelings. Every family will have its own values and ideas about sexual behavior, and the beliefs of your religion, family, and culture are good guides. Listen also to your thoughts about your feelings. Ultimately, you decide what is right about sex and how much you want to act upon your feelings. Like most other temptations, sex has consequences, and you need to consider the risks of unwanted pregnancies and sexually transmitted diseases, as well as your beliefs and those of your family.

What do you think is the right age to start dating? There are two kinds of dates: group dates with a bunch of girls and guys who are not necessarily paired off, and single dating. Single dating is usually more serious then a bunch of friends going to a movie together. If you begin single dating much before the age of sixteen, you are more likely to get serious, go steady, and have sexual relations at a young age. You would also be more likely to marry young or marry due to an unplanned pregnancy. Many teenage brides are pregnant at their wedding. Young married couples often find it hard to cope with being parents when they are only young teens themselves. The best suggestion is to take dating, sex, and going steady very, very slowly. No one who really loves you wants to see you being forced into an adult role when you should be enjoying just being a teen.

Deciding whether you like someone is often hard. You might appreciate his clothes, his skills on the soccer field, or his eyes,

Deciding if you like someone takes time.

lips, or hair. But how do you know if you like all of him? A girl needs to spend time talking with a boy, finding common interests, and finding out how she feels about him and how he feels about her. Trying to make someone care for you or starting rumors that he likes you are tactics that will backfire in your face, and you may suffer great embarrassment. Instead, be honest, and ask if he cares about you or if he just wants to be friends. If he says he cares about you, then spend time getting to know all you can about each other. Does he want to spend more time with his friends and avoid you? If so, look around for someone else.

There should never be tolerance of abuse no matter how much you like each other. Does this boy verbally abuse you, or does anything he says frighten you? Yes to either question means good-bye, guy. Besides, would you really like him if he constantly put you down or made you feel emotionally beaten? And if he stalks you at school, at home, or on the phone, get your parents involved and seek help from the police. Some guys can be very freaky and make you feel uneasy.

Assuming that he passes these tests, think about whether the two of you are compatible. To be a couple, you should share similar values and education goals, and you should have similar feelings about responsibility to each other, your families, and your communities. Each of you should respect the other and the need you each have for time with friends, with family, or just to be alone.

In speaking with a marriage counselor in Virginia, I asked how often teen marriages make it for the long stretch, and how often they end early and bitterly. I was told that the statistics vary by culture, geographic regions, and the specific ages of the couples.

However, even with these considerations, "teen marriages rarely last more than a few years, because teens change a great deal each year and often do not grow in the same directions. This growing apart and money problems are the main reasons that teen marriages end and do so on a very bitter note."

In the March 1999 issue of *Life* magazine, teens were asked how they had learned about sex and sexual risks. One young man said he got a talk from his dad but had actually learned about HIV from a television interview of Magic Johnson discussing his HIV diagnosis. This young man said that no one actually tells guys or girls how to have sex, meaning the mechanics of making love. He felt that the only way to learn was by looking at porno movies! Please don't get involved with a guy who thinks sex is like a porno movie. Couples who date for long periods of time are often assumed to be having sex with each other. Yet many boys do not press girlfriends into having sex.

What Does an Expert Say?

Ms. Annette Robbin, a seventh-grade guidance counselor in San Diego, California, advises girls on issues of dating and getting along with all types of students. Robbin feels three concerns are important to most girls: race, role models, and violence.

Robbin works in a big-city school system and has students from every ethnic group. "If you walk into the lunchroom, you see groups of students clustered together. However, the races rarely mix, and each group has its own territory and groups of tables." Robbin notes, "Race seems to continue to be a concern of teens" in dating and in friendships. The article from *Life* magazine gave statistics on racial prejudice that distressed her. "Approximately 15 percent of whites said they were prejudiced against blacks, and 14.1 percent of blacks felt the same about whites. In interviews with the teens, they all agreed that groups tend not to mix. Having friends and dating people of another race is considered difficult." These numbers seemed to fit what Robbin observes. "It bothers me that after so many years and efforts by educators, students still can decide to hate simply due to skin color."

To try to make a difference in her school, Robbin invites a mixture of students to a group meeting every Friday morning. She attempts to have them learn that there is no need for hate and that they actually have many things in common with each other. The students write confidential journal entries for Robbin telling if they have changed their minds or feelings of hatred due to the group sessions. "So far," informs Robbin, "about 10 percent of the five hundred students who have attended say they have changed or would at least think about being friendly with other races at school." We should not forget that 85 percent of the black and the white teens believed they were not prejudiced.

In individual counseling sessions with her students, Robbin asks girls who they use as a role model. "Many girls said that their greatest role model was their mother. Girls tell me that they first think their mothers know nothing about issues that are important

SITUATION
Your friends dare you to shoplift.

GOOD CHOICE
Don't! This is theft and you could be arrested, or your photo circulated to other stores and you could be banned from a mall.

Friendships with people of other racial, religious, and ethnic backgrounds can enrich your life and your understanding of the world.

to young teens. Yet by the end of ninth grade, girls are beginning to realize that their mothers went through the same problems and insecurities as they do. They realized that mothers are very often right about most stuff."

The third issue Robbin hears about in her counseling is that of the acceptance of the high level of violence in public schools. "Many of the young teens had horror stories involving guns and knives. Some attended schools where lockers were checked daily for weapons and students had to pass through metal detectors to get to homeroom. Going to school in fear makes learning extremely hard."

What Do Parents Think?

Today's parents think teens are not much different from their own generation. Parents wish teens would fight less with each other and be more helpful around the house. Homework, grades, dating too young, and having a steady boyfriend are also concerns of the parents.

Yet most teens will tell you straight out that they are different in many ways. Today's teens have to deal with the realities of AIDS, gang violence, date rape, eating disorders, self-mutilation, suicide, and other fears that earlier generations knew little about. Many girls wish first of all that their parents would be less judgmental about their friends and less rigid about dating. They also want to be given praise when they behave responsibly instead of having only their faults pointed out.

Girls between the ages of ten and fourteen can seem unpredictable. This is a trait that parents find difficult to understand and cope with. But girls of today deal with an amazing number of issues, and the emotional roller-coasters they ride seem to be the way young teens react to life. Parents can help more if they stop pointing fingers and instead try to understand what a girl's life is like. Parents are good at promoting dialogue. Most girls want respect, compassion, and a nonjudgmental hearing of themselves and their friends.

Robbin reminds the parents of her students that "grown-ups need to challenge the minds of young teens, appreciate their hectic and difficult school hours, and give as much admiration and outright love as is possible. Only these emotions and actions can send a message that a young, female teen is not alone, is loved, and has the ability to make the right choices for her life."

Sex Is Not a Game

DON'T

Life growing in me
I think about you
And every day I wonder
Who will you be?
And every day I wonder
What will I do?
And every day I wonder
Will you hate me?
And every day I pray
That you won't be.

MOLLY IS FOURTEEN years old and tends to have extended, colorful dreams. One night she had a dream in which she was seventeen years old and had a special boyfriend. In her dream, Molly knew she had no wish to be a mother. How could she when she still needed her own mom for so much?

A pregnant teen faces hard decisions.

As with many science experiments in school, mistakes happen. Condoms are not one-hundred-percent effective in stopping sperm from reaching an egg. In her dream, Molly found herself pregnant after one sexual encounter with her boyfriend. He went off to college and never knew about the baby and dropped out of her life. As her dream continued, Molly faced her parents and said she was determined that this was meant to be her baby. Days and then weeks and finally two months passed. Molly had lost weight from throwing up, her grades were poor, and she felt like death. Her family discussed her options. She could keep the baby and attend a community college part time. A second possible decision would be to have the baby, miss a semester of school and then allow an adoption agency to find the child a good home. As she slept, Molly finally decided on the only other choice, an abortion. But when she went to the doctor, her embarrassment was extremely hard to deal with. So Molly left, even though her friends tried to talk her into going through with it. When her alarm finally rang, Molly woke up with a terrible headache and a chilled feeling from head to toe.

The Experts Answer Some Common Questions

Most girls think they'll never have to make a decision about an unwanted pregnancy. However, only total abstinence (no sex at all) can guarantee that you won't get pregnant. About 7 percent of American women aged fifteen to seventeen get pregnant every single year.

Q. What is an abortion?

A. Abortion means purposely ending a pregnancy before birth. Nearly 40 percent of adolescent pregnancies are ended by an abortion.

Q. Males and females who don't want to get sexually involved are sometimes teased. How can I handle that?

A. There is no reason to answer your friends if they ask about your sexual experience. This is a private matter, and none of their business. Your choice at this time may be not to have sex. This is a moral choice. Those who get involved with sex prior to understanding or feeling mature enough to handle it are the foolish ones.

Q. Why is everyone talking about sexually transmitted disease?

A. The incidence of sexually transmitted diseases has risen in the last 10 years as more teens have sex at an earlier age. And doctors have learned more about the long term possible effects—such as increased risks of HIV and other serious infections, and difficulty conceiving a child.

Q. Television sometimes shows women being forced to have sex by their husbands or lovers. Is that rape?

A. Any time there is force by a male to make a female comply it is rape. Yes, if your husband or boyfriend insists and pushes himself onto you while you say no, it is rape. If any male family member or family friend starts to behave in a way that makes you feel uncomfortable or threatened, talk about it with a parent or other relative who can take control of the situation before it

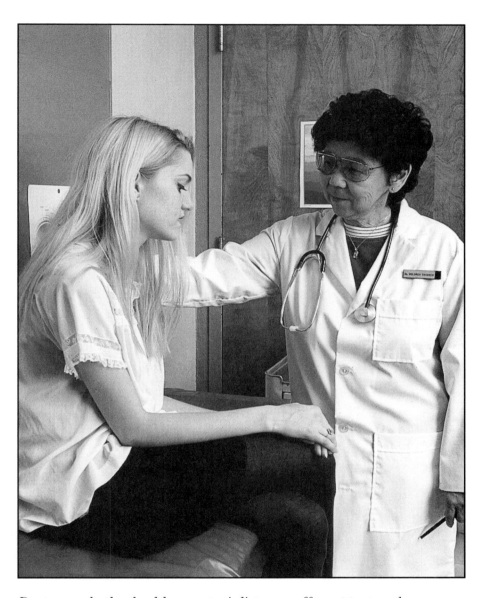

Doctors and other health care specialists can offer support and guidance, and the medical attention important for both the mother and the child.

gets out of hand. If they won't or can't help, go to a trusted teacher or counselor. If you need more help, go to the police.

Q. Why don't teenage girls think about the risk of getting pregnant?

A. Most teens think they are not at risk even when they are being risk-takers. But they find out when it is too late that they are not immune to the results of poor choices. Even today, though birth-control methods have improved, the risks are real. Some girls may think of abortion as an easy way out if things go wrong. But is it an easy out? There are significant financial, physical, and emotional costs.

Q. Do girls have sex just because people say "everyone" is doing it?

A. There is a lot of peer pressure about sexual behavior. In truth, however, if you realize that fifty percent of girls at age seventeen are still virgins, it means a lot of talking is going on about things that are not happening.

Q. Is the pill a good choice for birth control? Does it always protect?

A. Approximately ten percent of teens on the pill get pregnant during the first year that they are using it. And, as with any medication, there are risks and side effects.

Q. How many girls actually do get pregnant?

A. Studies show that one out of three sexually active teen girls gets pregnant outside of marriage. Maybe girls choosing to be active need to think about what they will do *when* they get pregnant and not just *if*.

Q. Is it true that if you don't have a condom or other birth control, plastic wrap will work?

A. How often have you taken a bowl of fruit or soup covered with plastic wrap out of the refrigerator only to have it leak or spill onto the floor? Plastic wrap has microscopic holes, it tears very easily, and it will come off at the worst time. This isn't a reliable method. Remember, sperm are mobile and were made to swim up to fertilize an egg—plastic wrap can't control that!

Q. What about watching the calendar and avoiding sex when you are ovulating (when the egg is making its way through the fallopian tubes)?

A. This method of birth control has been used throughout the world for centuries. There is nothing wrong with it for people who can deal with unexpected babies. It is really too difficult to time ovulation exactly, and sperm can live inside of you for several hours, or even days.

Q. Can you get pregnant from sexual activity without actual intercourse?

A. Actually you can. A pretty heavy session can lead to a male having an ejaculation (when matter made of semen comes out of his penis) outside your body. If your bodies are close enough, it is possible that a sperm could enter your body. There are usually between 100 million and 500 million sperm ejaculated each time, so one sperm could reach an egg.

This brief sample of questions about sex only scratches the surface of a large, important subject. Your school or public library has shelves full of books to provide answers. You can also search the Internet under "health" and then "sex" to find more information.

Having a Baby

If you are pregnant, the first thing to do is to go to a doctor or clinic to make sure you are doing everything you need to do to take care of yourself and your baby. If you need help finding where to go, there are hotlines and other resources listed at the end of this book, and in the yellow pages under Pregnancy Information Services. If you plan to keep your baby, find out about prenatal classes, parenting classes, and other sources of help.

The decision of how to handle an unplanned pregnancy is one of the most important choices you may ever need to make. You need to think it through. Help is available from many sources—religious advisories, Planned Parenthood, mental health and social service organizations, and parents. There is no one right choice. It has to be the right (or the best) choice for you. No one should pressure you into making the choice they think is right.

Many young pregnant girls choose to keep their babies. Dr. Karen Green, a pediatrician, offers some basic instructions on a healthy baby. She reminds readers that "loving your child is your most important task for your baby. Responsibility for the baby's well-being is next, and adjusting your life to being a mother is third.

SITUATION
A classmate, teacher, or someone sexually harasses you physically or verbally.

GOOD CHOICE
Make it clear that you don't like this. If it continues, talk to a parent, counselor, principal, or police.

68

"New babies are very expensive and time-consuming and they tend to make you grow up very fast. Among teens, a higher percentage of the pregnancies occur among girls in their mid and upper teens, but sadly we are seeing girls as young as twelve purposely getting pregnant and trying to raise their babies." Dr. Green adds that for many young girls, "having a baby gives the feeling of having something all your own to love. Although this sounds at first to be tender-hearted, it is actually selfish. A baby is not a live doll, and babies should not be born to make the mother feel special."

What a Police Officer Wants You to Know

Officer Claire Stein is a police officer in New York City who works with many teens who have new babies. Officer Stein watchs out for newborns. "I want to be sure that the mothers are given a chance to get off the street, or that there are grandparents to help to keep the baby healthy. Girls need to think of health issues for their baby's safety. During pregnancy, do not drink alcohol or smoke cigarettes, and certainly stay away from drugs. Every one of these can be a real danger to your baby's brain development and size. It can also add to or cause such learning problems as Attention Deficit Hyperactivity Disorder [ADHD]. Having ADHD will make learning in school more of a challenge for your child. Your bad habits may also cause your child to be hyperactive. When a child is hyperactive, he or she can be aggressive and hit other classmates or have difficulty staying seated. It's also important not to take up smoking or other habits once you bring your baby home. Breathing in smoke all day is not good for you or your child."

If you are returning to live at home, try to do the work yourself with help from the father of the baby. Your parents have already done baby duty and should not be expected to raise your child. A representative of a school system in New York City who works with young mothers and helps them to return to school offers this advice for new teen mothers: "Don't expect your life to go back to the way it was. When your stomach is flat again, you still have a baby who is dependent on you for at least eighteen years. Starting off smart will make it easier in later years. Be certain to give your baby attention." Officer Stein says that many girls make mistakes that hurt their babies. Knowing the right way to care for a newborn is very important. She wants new mothers to know that:

- "You do not just put a baby to sleep on the couch and spend the day polishing your nails. Every nap time, your baby should be in her crib, and you should rest or do your housework and schoolwork."
- "Most school systems throughout the country have facilities for young mothers to return and finish their school requirements."
- "Shaken baby syndrome is caused by hard shaking of a baby. Shaking for even for a couple of seconds can cause bleeding into and around the baby's brain. This can destroy brain cells and cause loss of vision, brain damage, paralysis, vomiting, seizures, and even death."

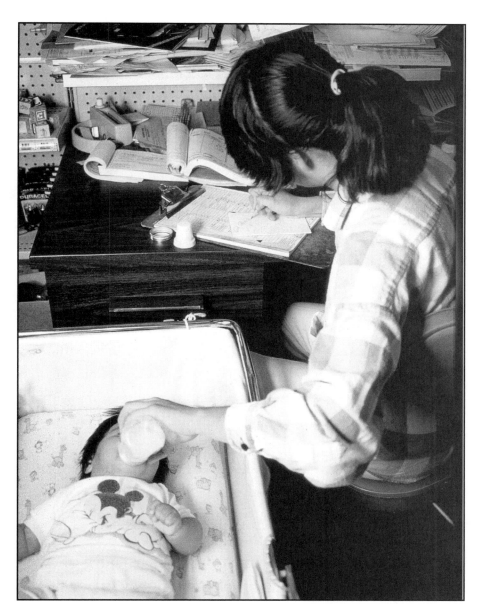

A teen mother tries to balance schoolwork and child care.

There is a great deal more you need to know: how and when to feed and bathe the baby, when you need a doctor, what to do when the baby cries, and the answers to a million other questions. Books, parenting classes, and mother and child support groups are all helpful.

Young mothers can get worn to a frazzle. Going to school, working, or getting a GED and then caring for a baby is exhausting. It is hard for mothers to stay calm when a baby cries for a long time. When your baby cries, you should check her diaper and try to calm her. She might be hungry or tired. If a baby won't stop crying, a person may lose control and shake the baby to make the crying stop. At all times and at all costs, do not do this, as your baby will never be the same.

Remember that you are not all alone. Call a friend; most will be happy to keep you company or stay with your baby while you nap. Find a way to get rid of your stress. Run, garden, scrub a floor, write letters—whatever you need to do to calm yourself. And *never* discipline your baby while you are angry. That could lead to abuse.

There are four types of child abuse. **Physical abuse** includes slapping, beating, starving, and other cruel behaviors. The signs and symptoms include cuts, burns, bite marks, broken bones, fear of adults, and problems at school. **Emotional abuse**—mocking, disrespect, verbal cruelty, emotional deprivation—often results in depression, stress, eating disorders, and hopelessness. **Sexual abuse** includes using a child for sexual purposes. Signs of sexual abuse include an unusual interest or knowledge of sexual acts. Other symptoms are nightmares, bed-wetting, change in appetite, aggression, and suicidal thoughts or gestures. **Neglect** is another form of abuse. It involves lack of attention to proper dressing, feeding and bathing, and supervision.

If you decided to put your baby up for adoption, you know that such a decision can be very painful. Adoption agencies often work with the biological (birth) mother to help her make a decision that she feels is the right one for her. One social worker who works with birth mothers notes that "what you might think of as a loss will be the answer to another couple's life-long dream of having a baby." An unknown poet wrote this poem about adopted children:

LEGACY OF AN ADOPTED CHILD

Once there were two women who never knew each other,
One you do not remember, the other you call Mother.
Two different lives shaped to make you one
One became your guiding star, the other became your sun.
The first one gave you life and the second taught you how to live it.
The first gave you a need for love, the second was there to give it.
One gave you a nationality, the other gave you a name.
One gave you a talent, the other gave you aim.
One gave you emotions, the other dried your tears.
One sought for you a home that she could not provide, the other prayed for a child and her hope was not denied.
And now you ask me through your tears,
the age-old question, unanswered through the years.
Heredity or environment, which are you a product of?
Neither my darling, neither.
Just two different kinds of love.

Sexual Identity

Another concern for some teens is sexual identity or orientation. A counselor advises that the teen years are a confusing time and young people may experience feelings of heterosexuality (a desire for a male-female relationship), homosexuality (a desire for a same-sex relationship), or bisexuality (a desire for a relationship with a male or a female). These may be phases in the process of sexual discovery.

Sexual identity is a private, individual matter. It takes time to know and understand your sexual nature as well as any other aspect of who you are. It is important to avoid hasty decisions and commitments and to resist any efforts to talk you into a decision for which you are unprepared. SIECUS, the Sexuality Information and Education Council of the United States (*http://www.siecus.org*), your doctor, and the library (look up "sexuality") are good sources of information.

This chapter has looked at a range of issues: sex, pregnancy, child raising, and dangers to your baby. Saying no to sex or practicing safer sex are your best options. Before making choices, you need to have information to help you deal with your feelings and the situations so that you are able to make good choices.

You Can Be at Risk

HELP

I see you struggling by the side of the road
I see you begging to make ends meet
I see you hopeless and forlorn but
I walk past you, drop a nickel in your cup
Put my blinders on, reassure myself that I've
done what I can
I watch you selling yourself to buy bread
I watch you sleeping on a bed of last week's paper
I watch you despair and give up on your life
But I tell myself that there's nothing I can do
That it's not my place, not my problem
And then I remember not too long ago
I was the one giving up, a few pennies in my cup
Where would I be now if someone hadn't stopped,
Stepped down and given me a chance?

STEPHANIE IS FIFTEEN years old and her cousin Sharon is thirteen. The girls are close friends and often spend weekends at each other's homes. They play computer games, talk about boys, and watch TV. With a big bag of popcorn and the phone right next to them, they spend hours just enjoying being with each other. Their mothers are sisters, and the girls have grown up together. There is nothing that one girl can't tell the other, and they help each other with every problem.

One weekend, Stephanie was unusually quiet. Every time Sharon asked if she was okay, her cousin would just shrug her shoulders. Finally, late that night, Stephanie asked if she could get in bed with Sharon as they did when they were little. Sharon pulled back her covers so that her cousin could climb in. Once they were comfortable, Stephanie began to cry. Sharon put her arms around her and asked to please be told the secret. Stephanie slowly told Sharon the whole story.

Stephanie's new boyfriend is very popular at school. She thinks he is so cute and is excited that he likes her. When they went to the movies last weekend, he put his arm around her and told her he liked her as a special girlfriend. After the movie, they went to his friend's house. There was a small party going on in the backyard, but Stephanie and her boyfriend went up to his friend's bedroom. Stephanie liked kissing and even liked having her boyfriend caress her. It didn't take long for them to start taking off clothing, and Stephanie said that before she realized it, she was making love. Although it scared her, she felt very grown-up and not at all embarrassed. But now Stephanie was starting to worry.

It is often hard to deal with serious problems alone.

What if she got pregnant? What if he had AIDS? Could she catch other diseases?

Sharon hugged her tight and said it would be a good idea to ask her mom for some answers. The girls put on robes and woke up Sharon's mom. They all went into the kitchen, and Stephanie told her story again. Her aunt was so calm and gentle that Stephanie felt better and was able to discuss the problem and find out what she needed to do for her health and safety.

When Stephanie went home on Sunday, her mom was not angry. She just wanted to help Stephanie. They decided that Stephanie should go to see her pediatrician on Monday and talk to her.

What Do the Experts Say?

By Monday afternoon, Stephanie was getting nervous, but she had known the doctor all her life and really liked and trusted her. Dr. Jenny Alstrom listened to Stephanie and told her that "she was smart to come in for a checkup. Since Stephanie did not know if her boyfriend had sex before, it was important to have some tests to be sure her health was fine." Since Stephanie was only fifteen, the doctor said either she could examine Stephanie, or she would help her make an appointment with a gynecologist. This kind of doctor deals with female issues and examines the pelvic area (this includes your sex organs, bladder, liver, and other organs in the area of the lower abdomen).

Stephanie said she preferred having Dr. Alstrom check her out. Dr. Alstrom says "If a girl is sexually active, a pelvic exam should take place at least once a year, and two times a year would be better. It is important to check for sexually transmitted diseases [STDs] that need to be treated with medication. Sexually transmitted diseases can cause problems with being able to have a baby when you are ready to start a family." Even more worrisome is the threat of AIDS.

Stephanie was starting to worry again, but Dr. Alstrom told her the exam would not take long, and "all we do after the pelvic exam is take some blood to send to the lab. We'll know the results by the end of the week. Don't worry, you are probably fine," added Dr. Alstrom. By Friday, Stephanie knew her results were clear. She will return for another test in six months to be sure. She also broke up with her boyfriend. Stephanie realized that she was frightened and not ready to deal with a sexual relationship.

Not every female is as lucky as Stephanie. Many diseases are transmitted through unprotected sex (not using a condom.) HIV, the virus that causes AIDS, is transmitted through unprotected sex and by partners who may not know that they are carriers of HIV or STDs or may not tell

SITUATION
You think someone is following you, or stalking you.

GOOD CHOICE
Go into a store or a police or fire station and ask for help. Call a parent to come and meet you. Being stalked is not a joke. Get the police involved.

the truth about their health, notes Dr. Alstrom. The same is true for other STDs. For more information on birth-control methods, pregnancy, the effects of the birth-control pill, and STDs, look up Birth Control and Contraception for Teenagers on the Internet at *www.avert.org/cpills.htm* and in your library.

Advice from a Special Nurse

Susan Wertheim is an AIDS researcher who lives in Dallas, Texas. Trained as a nurse who has worked with dying cancer patients, Wertheim recently began studying AIDS and working with a group of doctors who hope to find a cure. "AIDS [acquired immunodeficiency syndrome] and HIV, which causes AIDS, are easily transmitted through unprotected sex. HIV is a virus that attacks the T-cells of your immune system. These cells help fight off disease. As the T-cells become infected or die off, your body has less and less ability to protect itself. Infections begin to appear. At this point you may have AIDS," explains Wertheim. "Early intervention is vital. Getting tested is the very first thing to do. If the test comes back as HIV negative, the patient does not seem to be infected with the virus." A follow-up test in six months can confirm this. However, Wertheim shouted, "USE CONDOMS ANYWAY!"

Wertheim continues: "If the test report comes back as HIV positive or asymptomatic, it means the patient has been exposed to the virus. Getting medical help immediately can mean adding years to the patient's life. By accepting and dealing with the fact that one has a disease, the person can stay healthier. Many people have lived more than ten years without experiencing symptoms." Ms.Wertheim explains that the disease is not easy to understand and is being studied to find out why some people live for many years and others die quickly. "Anyone exposed to the disease should educate herself. Find out about support groups and new trends in medication; choose a doctor with HIV experience; keep nutrition up; decide which, if any, people will be told; and deter-

Education is an important defense against AIDS. Here high school girls talk to middle school girls about HIV transmission.

mine the type of treatment desired. Discuss all of the options with your doctor," advises Wertheim.

If a girl fears that she might have been infected or wishes to be sure that she is clear, "she can get an AIDS blood test," says Wertheim. "This will give a person piece of mind. Any partner should do the same. Do not just believe a boy who says he has never had sex before or that all his partners were disease free. Insist on tests, and insist on condoms, even if both people are disease free."

We can't always know whether someone has AIDS. Signs of the illness are weight loss, frequent colds and coughs, sores that don't heal, and extreme loss of energy, but not everyone with AIDS or HIV has symptoms. Medicines can prolong life, but there is no cure yet, and many AIDS patients face a long, painful illness and a dreadful death.

When HIV first appeared in North America, it was most common among homosexuals. Since 1985, the epidemic has spread among drug users, and among heterosexuals and in the African-American and Latino populations. In recent years the greatest increases are among women and teens. For reasons that are not yet clear, AIDS is spreading quickly in the southern part of the United States. The number of cases in Washington, D.C., is also quite high. These changes in the pattern of AIDS are one of the subjects of Wertheim's research.

Wertheim points out that "there have not been many newspaper or TV programs about HIV and AIDS recently. Teens are not getting enough information to be safe. Although you can't get AIDS by touching someone who has it, you can get it from the person's infected blood or body fluids mixing with yours. Two ways to get infected are by having unprotected sex, and sharing drug needles."

Susan Wertheim has an important job in the fight to find a cure for AIDS. She is in charge of clinical trials that determine whether a drug is approved by the government for use in the

United States. Any medication developed by a pharmaceutical (drug) company is carefully tested before it is offered to the public, and getting a new drug approved can take eight to ten years.

There are four steps to a clinical trial. First, the drug is tested on animals. Next, the drug is tested on a set of animals and some humans. In the third step, the drug is given to humans to determine the best dosage. And finally, a fourth trial looks at whether the drug causes any harmful side effects. Usually, the people who agree to be part of a clinical trial have the disease and want to help find a cure. Wertheim's office staff includes a doctor who, along with the drug company, is the principal investigator in the study and monitors the study along with Wertheim. "It is important for people to know," says Wertheim, "that people with AIDS are now living for a much longer time. The drugs that are currently approved and being used are prolonging the lives of many patients. However, a cure is still needed, and young women need to be careful. Casual sex is too dangerous, and unprotected sex is just plain stupid."

What About Other Diseases?

There are other STDs that girls need to learn about. Each can cause problems, and most can be treated with medication.

Chlamydial infection is the most common sexually transmitted bacterial disease in teens from fifteen to nineteen. It may cause genital discharge and burning during urination. If not treated, it may lead to pelvic inflammatory disease and is a major cause of women being unable to have children. A male may have no symptoms, yet may be carrying and spreading the infection.

Genital herpes affects 60 million Americans and is characterized by painful blisters or open sores on the genital area. It is not curable but is controllable by medication. The blisters will usually go away in two to three weeks, but the virus stays in your body. If a woman has active herpes while giving birth, it can cause mental retardation in her baby.

Genital warts are caused by a virus (human papilloma virus) that is related to the virus that causes skin warts. Up to 4 million new cases a year are found among young people. The warts first appear as small, hard, painless bumps on the vaginal area. If left untreated, they grow quite large and can be painful. They are usually removed by freezing them, or other treatments in a doctor's office, or by surgery. They may return and may be infectious.

Gonorrhea can cause painful urination and discharge from the vagina. Combinations of drugs such as penicillin and other antibiotics are the treatment. Prompt treatment is very important. Untreated, this STD can cause infertility (the inability to have children) in women, chronic pain, and other problems.

Syphilis is a little tricky to diagnose. It is referred to as the "great imitator" because its early stages look like symptoms of less serious diseases. The initial symptom is a painless open sore on the vaginal area, or on the lips or inside the mouth. This quickly heals and goes away. Later symptoms include flulike feelings, enlarged glands, a body rash. If the disease is untreated, this STD can progress to a dreadful conclusion. At a late stage the central nervous system (brain, spinal cord, nerves) is affected. Syphilis can be cured by prompt treatment with antibiotics.

Other STDs include several vaginal viruses, scabies (a disease of the skin caused by mites that live under the skin and cause itching), and lice in the pubic hair. All STDs can hurt

Schools, libraries, clinics, and other health care facilities provide information about safer sex, birth control, AIDS, and other STDs.

newborns and unborn babies and can cause serious complications such as spontaneous abortion (miscarriage) or mental retardation. Permanent neurological damage, pneumonia, low body weight, premature births, and infected newborns are also possibilities. An essential fact to remember when you are making an intelligent decision about becoming sexually active is that the younger you start, the more susceptible you become to STDs. Also, since some STDs cause no visible symptoms in females, it is important for all sexually active females to have regular check-ups (once or twice a year) with a gynecologist or other health care specialist.

Every one of the described STDs sounds disgusting and makes a strong case for the use of condoms. You always have the right and the choice to ask a male to use a condom. A female condom can also be used. This condom covers the vagina and the cervix, and protects against pregnancy and STDs. If he does not go along with your informed choice, show him out.

"When it comes to sex," Dr. Alstrom warns, "always choose safety over acting like the 'in crowd' or being popular."

Every girl needs to remember that she can say no, she can change her mind, and she can refuse sexual overtures or decide not to make them. Examine your feelings about sex, and set limits that make you comfortable. After all, it is your body and your decision. Be certain that the person you are involved with knows your feelings about sex. That usually means you need to talk about them. If you are not eager for sex, try not to give mixed signals. Saying yes with your actions and no with your mouth sends signals that you do not intend. Yes means yes, and no means no, and stick to that. Be firm and forceful if necessary. Acknowledge that a situation may be dangerous, and follow your gut reactions. Finally, if things start to get out of control, be loud in protesting, leave, go for help, or call home.

Remember, making choices that keep us safe is part of growing up female. You always have the choice to leave, no matter how much your date complains.

Respect Yourself

7

I CAME TO MYSELF

At the end of my journey through life,
I came to a harsh conclusion.
Things are how you believe them to be,
Your thoughts are in reality.
Thought peers out at you, haunting you,
Watching your every move and criticizing.
The same reality frightens fairies,
What you believe may be a fantasy.
The journey has put many sores on my feet,
Yet many visions in my head of a clear path.

WHEN SUSAN LOOKS at herself, she sees a fat girl. Her friends and family think she looks great, and boys think she is very nice looking. Susan cannot believe them. The summer before seventh grade, Susan began to feel self-conscious in a bathing suit and stopped going to the community pool. She decided to lose weight during the school year so she could look "right" in her clothes and next year's swimsuit. She began by cutting out all junk food. Then she ate only two small meals a day. She drank water for lunch.

A counselor works with a teen suffering from an eating disorder, and tries to help the patient correct her distorted body image.

Even though her grades began to drop, Susan didn't see a need to eat lunch. Every time she passed by a mirror or a store window, she would still see the "fat girl" she believed herself to be. Drastic cuts in her food consumption made her feel thinner. So did riding her bike for two hours a day. But she began to look dreadful to everyone else.

Her mother tried to get Susan to go to her doctor or seek other help. She told Susan she was too skinny and looked like a sack of bones. But Susan's mother was an "outsider," a person who, unlike Susan, does not have an eating disorder, and she cannot help by making delicious food or praising Susan if she eats. Susan's frantic dieting is an emotionally based disorder involving body-image and control issues, and only good therapy, support groups, and Susan's making the choice to eat will save her life.

Parents need to take a strong stand when a girl has an eating problem. The girl cannot handle her feelings and make reasonable decisions herself. Sometimes being hospitalized for a recovery period is a necessary approach.

The years of middle school and high school can bring tremendous pressure and pain as girls like Susan struggle with their appearance and their wish to fit into the currently popular "skinny girl" look. With television, movies, and fashion magazines showing ultrathin women as desirable, girls often develop a skewed view of what is attractive.

Eating is one of life's pleasures, yet girls whose body image tells them they are fat go to great lengths to make their bodies look different. There is a tendency during the teen and preteen ages to feel out of control. The eating disorder anorexia is an attempt to gain control in at least one area of one's life—the appetite.

Food provides us with the fuel to run our bodies and brains, and with the satisfaction of feeling full, not hungry. For some young women, eating is not a simple pleasure but rather a complex set of rituals that mean "I am good, so I deserve food," or "I am bad, so I can't eat." These rituals may include starving, bingeing, purging, and even overeating. Females suffer from these eating disorders in greater numbers than males. But due to growing awareness of these eating problems, more help is now available to girls.

Robin Marsh of CBS Television Health Watch recommends that girls who are concerned about compulsive eating practices realize that they are not alone and that help is available through the Internet in several forms. You can read pamphlets from the National Institute of Mental Health online. Good articles can be found on the Mayo Clinic's Health Oasis website. And finally, a terrific website is the Something Fishy website on eating disorders. You can find an amazing variety of articles and information there (*www.something-fishy.org/ed-1.htm*).

Dr. Lucas of the Mayo Clinic points out that "Anorexia nervosa occurs in up to one percent of girls aged thirteen to seventeen, peaking at girls aged fifteen. If not treated, anorexia can lead to serious physical problems such as malnutrition, damage to the heart and kidneys, and even death." A girl may also lose bone

SITUATION
You are asked to join a gang.

GOOD CHOICE
Be careful! Think about who the members are and what they do. Are members controlled, or forced to do things that are illegal or could hurt someone? Remember that if you join a gang, it might be hard to drop out.

density, which leads to arthritis and brittle bones later in life. Anemia and infertility can also result.

An anorexic may become skilled at denying or disguising her behavior. She may become crafty at moving food around a plate so it looks as if some of it has been eaten. She may avoid being around at mealtimes, or claim to have just eaten. The anorexic will wear layers of clothing to look a normal size and not arouse suspicion.

Bulimia nervosa, often called bingeing and purging, is an eating disorder in which girls eat large amounts of high-calorie food in a short amount of time. They then use vomiting or laxatives to rid their bodies of the food before the body can digest it. This disorder is actually more common than anorexia nervosa. Bulimia nervosa occurs in two to four percent of girls in their mid to late teens.

Bulimics usually don't gain or lose large amounts of weight, but the disorder still causes severe damage to the body. Frequent vomiting brings stomach acid into the mouth, causing damage to teeth and gums. That is why dentists are often the first to notice the problem in a female patient. Other health problems caused by bingeing and purging include dehydration, lack of important minerals in the body, and damage to vital body organs. Dr. Mary Ann Bauman, who specializes in treating eating disorders, warns that other medical problems can occur, including "tears of the stomach . . . pneumonia and tears of the lungs . . . difficulty with thinking, memory, and depression." Her website, *drbauman@ kwtv.com*, offers more information.

One of the differences between the two eating disorders is that girls with anorexia usually do not think they have a problem. They feel proud to have such control over their appetites. But actually they have no choice but to starve themselves. What must be emphasized is that they have surrendered choice—they are victims of their will gone wild. Dr. Lucas adds, "On the other hand, teens and young women with bulimia often realize that they have a problem and become depressed after binges." Dr. Lucas reminds parents that these conditions—anorexia and bulimia—are serious and need to be taken seriously. However it is true that teenagers often have unusual eating habits. Minor deviations are normal, and changes aren't always danger signals.

There are some signs that will indicate that a girl has an eating problem:

- Is her weight decreasing during a time of growth, when she should be gaining weight?
- Does she think she is fat no matter how much weight she loses?
- Does she manage to be a high achiever but has low self-esteem?
- Does she seem to need to say no to eating in order to have control over her life?
- Does she hide her purges by running the water in the bathroom sink while spending long periods of time in the bathroom?

Another eating disorder is compulsive overeating. This is also very sad because the sufferer is often a young girl who is unsure

A sense of being excluded, or feeling unacceptable may contribute to the development of an eating disorder.

of her acceptance by others. Unfortunately, she makes that acceptance harder by gorging on food. Overeaters go on food frenzy binges. They eat their way through box after box of cookies. They eat enormous amounts of foods with high fat content. Fighting to control their body weight may become a lifetime obsession. These girls are feeding their fat cells at a time when the body is still developing. Compulsive overeating is used by a girl to fill a void or emptiness she strongly feels. She needs to learn that overeating will not fill that void.

Dieting is related to a girl's sense of herself. Eating disorders can start as a vanity issue. A concern about appearance then progresses when a girl uses food control as a coping mechanism for stress, a hatred or shame of herself, or a hurt that she has suffered.

If you want to help a friend with an eating disorder, here are some dos and don'ts to consider. Remember, if you are an "outsider," your friend may not want help or listen to you. You can only try to help.

Do

- gently encourage correct eating.
- express your concern, love, and support.
- try to understand and empathize with her problem.
- emphasize all of her good traits and compliment her.
- talk honestly and sincerely, with love and understanding.
- help her find support services and encourage her to talk to her family.
- recognize that a nonfood issue is the underlying cause.
- encourage her to express her feelings.

Don't

- try to make her eat or stop exercising.
- get angry or punish her with your actions.
- get impatient or lecture her.
- see things just through your eyes; look through hers too.

- spy on her or make her feel guilty.
- let her place the blame on others.
- be afraid to talk about her problems.
- pretend it will just go away.
- expect instant recovery.
- let her feel alone or that she is the only one to have this condition.

Most important: Do all that you can to convince your friend to get help from a therapist who specializes in eating disorders.

If you or a friend suffers from an overconcern about your weight, look for healthier and more effective methods of weight control and improving your self image rather than slipping into eating disorders. It is important to find the right method for you so that weight control is reasonable and safe. In many cases, girls carry a bit of extra weight while their bodies are developing. Then, after a growth spurt, the extra weight comes off naturally. Follow your doctor's advice; do not risk your health to fit into a certain size of jeans! And only try to lose weight if you want to, or if advised to by a health professional, not because someone else says you should. Check with a doctor to determine whether you do need to loose weight, and to plan your method. Then make a commitment to work at it.

Set your weight loss goals at a reasonable amount. Nearly 8 million Americans enroll in a weight-loss program each year. Trying to lose too much weight dooms them to failure, or the weight just comes back when the program is stopped.

SITUATION
A family member or a friend's brother or someone else has abused you.

GOOD CHOICE
It isn't your fault, and you need help! Find an adult who will listen and help you—a parent, teacher, counselor, clinic doctor, or police officer. You need medical attention, protection, and emotional support.

Healthy weight loss is slow and steady, and you should try to lose up to only one pound per week. It takes longer, but this type of dieting works and is not destructive. According to weight-control specialists at the Mayo Clinic (a research hospital that looks into many types of diseases), no one should eat fewer than 1,200 calories a day, and growing girls should consume more to maintain proper body development. The Mayo Clinic warns that cutting some of your fat intake is okay, but you need to eat essential nutrient-rich foods such as whole grains, vegetables, and fruits.

These same Mayo Clinic experts also indicate that dieting is not always as successful as changing your daily patterns. For example, taking a walk daily, going out for a sports team, avoiding second and third helpings at meals, and leaving the table when you feel full are excellent ways to shed a few pounds.

For middle-school girls, confidence in the way they look is vital. This is one of the main reasons any female who is slightly different is often made to feel that she is ugly or strange.

These eating disorders often develop because a girl desperately wants to feel accepted and worthwhile. She focuses this need on food and tries to control the one thing she can when everything else seems to be out of her power. Strangely, her need for acceptance leads to a disease that keeps her from the acceptance she craves and often spirals out of her control.

If family and friends can understand that a girl's weight is not the real issue, but an indicator of an internal struggle, and pain,

A counselor who once also had an eating disorder works with an anorexic teen.

they can start to help. Charlotte Stark writes for the website of the Mental Health Foundation in London, England. She suggests that any girl who thinks she has a problem with food should turn to "special organizations that give practical and emotional support for those experiencing eating disorders." She adds that what girls with eating disorders "need most is love and respect. They need constant reminders that they are valued for who they are and not what they look like."

Girls who suffer from eating disorders have an illness that should not be taken lightly or ignored. Treatment should include therapy, nutritional counseling, and medications if appropriate.

Relapse—going back to the eating disorder—is a constant danger. Support groups help to keep a girl from relapsing.

Recovery programs for girls (or women) with eating disorders focus on helping them to create a more normal relationship with food. To help girls reach their goals, recovery centers use group therapy, medical treatment, nutritional supplements when needed, and individual body image work. There are even online centers to help girls deal with eating disorders. And there are many books dealing with the subject. The "To Find Out More" section at the end of this book lists a few. Although there is no substitute for working one-on-one with a therapist, going online for information and suggestions of recovery centers is a good place to start. Jeanne Rust, a counselor in Arizona who specializes in eating disorders, is an online resource. Her Internet site is Eating Disorder Recovery Online (*jrust@edrecovery.com*).

After reading the information here and checking some websites and books, use what you learn to give yourself the courage to seek help if you have an eating disorder. Learning to find better ways to cope is not easy, but that will be a major part of your recovery. With the many emotional ups and downs of the middle school years, it is important that you find people you can trust who will listen to your concerns. Whether your concerns are about your home life and family or about kids at school, counseling or therapy will help you gain understanding and conquer your fears.

The Tyranny of Cliques 8

INSPIRED

I am inspired
But who do I inspire?
I am taught
But who do I teach?
I can hear
But who is heard by me?
I am loved
But whom have I loved?
I am watched
But what do my actions say?
I am
But who am I?

ONE OF THOSE parental questions that seem to have been handed down from generation to generation is, "If your friends jumped off the Empire State Building, would you jump too?" It is a symbolic question; no parent or caregiver expects you to say yes. However, generations of teens have seen what a group of girls can do when they band together. Most women when they were in middle school had some experience of pain caused by such a group of "best-best" friends who turned out not to be real friends. This experience made seventh grade a dreadful year for Marissa.

Tall, blonde, and good-hearted, with beautiful eyes and porcelain skin, Marissa had always attracted friends. Unlike some seventh graders who stuck only with their elementary-school friends or who hung out only with older kids, Marissa had friends in every group. She rarely made a big deal about people's looks, grades, race, or age. If you were honest, decent, and interested in the same things she thought were fun, she'd be your friend. At least her choices were made that way until seventh grade.

Marissa's style of dress was unusual. She liked punk bands and the way they dressed. Other girls would copy her. The new shoes she wore on a Monday would be on everyone's feet by Friday. Yet as popular and as influential as she was, Marissa never thought about it. The others were her friends, so they dressed alike. She didn't see herself as a leader, just as one of a group of girls.

A group of girls wanted Marissa to be friends only with them. She had to choose them and no one else, or never be friends with them again. As many of her friends were in this group, Marissa

The cruel power of a teenage clique

chose to stay with them. After three or four months of happy days and doing things together, a new girl, Rachel, moved into town, the school, and the group.

Rachel quickly worked herself into the group. She complimented everyone, thought up silly or sneaky things for them to do, and made Marissa feel like her best friend. One day after an assembly at school, Rachel talked the girls into taking a bus to the mall. They had very little money and weekday mall trips were not really O.K. with their parents. At a jewelry store, Rachel dared them each to steal something. Then they would wrap the treasures and give them to each other on Friday. That way no one's mother would think it was strange that her daughter had new earrings. All the girls in the group did it and felt very smart to get away with it. They told no one.

When Rachel suggested the next week that they go shoplifting in a music store, they all went. Only Marissa felt that the owner's eyes were on her. She couldn't make herself shoplift. As weeks went on, Rachel took more and more control over the girls. She even had everyone celebrate her birthday by having them wear similar clothes that day.

Teachers with years of school experience often say it's easier to describe what a clique is not, rather than what it is. It is not a club, nor a group formed by girls with similar interests that takes in new members. In Marissa's case, the girls appeared to be interested in fashion, but they really were not about that. A clique is a

SITUATION
You go to a party and see there are no adults home, and some students bring beer and drugs.

GOOD CHOICE
Find some other kids who don't like what's happening and leave together. Call a parent or Safe Rides to take you home.

very tightly bound group, with codes of behavior, and selective and exclusionary attitudes.

Mothers started comparing notes about the group. Rachel's mom thought it was cute that they all listened to her daughter. Only two moms asked, "Why is Rachel the boss?" As the girls became known as a special group, other kids at school started to call them snobs, freaks, Rachel wanna-bes, and sluts.

Rachel had a hold on the girls, mainly through fear, and she wanted to be the sole leader. She seemed to resent Marissa for her independence and to want her out of the group. Rachel began spreading lies about Marissa, and the other girls backed her up. They liked Marissa but would not risk being Rachel's victim. Marissa found a crumpled-up note on the floor near her locker. Rachel had written a list of seventh-grade guys and said that Marissa had kissed them all! No one asked whether the list could be true, nor did anyone try to help Marissa. On her mother's advice, Marissa decided to ignore Rachel and let the situation pass.

It wasn't long before the group started crowding around her in the gym locker and screaming awful things at her. This upset her and made her feel very sad. Next, they sang a song they had written called, "Rest in Peace, Marissa." This was scary and all she could handle. Saying nothing, she dressed and went home. In the darkness of a rainy Sunday, Marissa stared into space feeling lonely and heartbroken. She began to cry and picked up a scissors, mindlessly moving to make a cut on her knee. Marissa's mom just happened to look in on her then and took away the scissors. Dropping to the floor, Marissa's mom held her and sang her favorite

Being excluded may leave scars.

baby songs, making her feel loved. Eventually Marissa stopped crying. Then they talked.

Her mother talked about how hard it is being young, especially in a world made up of so many choices. You need to know right from wrong, and how to handle difficult situations, balance loyalties and honesty and authority and other forces. Marissa was terrified of going back to school. Whom would she eat lunch with? Who would be her new friends? That night, Marissa slept little, but she got on the bus when it stopped at her corner the next morning. It would be her first time facing Rachel since the song incident. No problem; Rachel ignored her, and Marissa sat near the driver. At school, classes were fine, but lunch was brutal. She was ignored or chased from lunch tables. A few girls from the soccer team asked her to sit with them. They told her everyone hated that group of girls because they acted as if they owned the school. Marissa was surprised at the comment and glad for the company. She started spending time with the members of the soccer team, and after a couple of weeks the coach asked to see her kick and run. Marissa's brother was a big soccer star, so she knew some rules and some tricks. The coach watched her dribble down the field and get the ball past their best goalie. The next week, the coach found a way to put her on the team. It would be only for three games, but practices took up all her empty time. She made it through school, her grades improved, and she discovered she had talent.

What Do the Experts Say?

Dr. Myra Burgee, a psychologist who works with young children and teenagers, has a lot to say about cliques. "The pain of dealing with a clique leaves scars on girls. The group members may not realize the effect they have and the psychological damage they cause. A clique, which often starts as early as third grade, has members who are actually insecure. Clique members bully others to build up their own self-esteem. The damage done by a clique can have long-time consequences, such as feeling socially awkward, or an outsider, or doubting one's own strength."

Rachel eventually moved on to another school. Marissa's former friends apologized, but she didn't like them very much or

Dressing alike, excluding and mocking others, provides clique members with a sense of belonging.

trust them any longer. Marissa had decided that real friends were better than a group held together by threats.

"How you handle the bullying makes a difference as to when and if it stops," Dr. Burgee notes. "Be brave and face it head on. Be proud of yourself and show only courage." Dr. Burgee says she wishes "teachers were better trained to spot these situations and to work with the students. Unfortunately, cliques are good at hiding what they are doing. You should try to face the clique but if the cruel treatment continues for more than a few weeks, you need help. Your parents need to know what is happening, and a change of schools may be necessary. Working with a school or private psychologist will help you understand why your 'friends' act this way and that you are a victim and it isn't your fault." They may have needed to find a victim to solidify their bonds, and you may have just been unlucky. Dr. Burgee adds a second point: "Adults would be fired from a job if they acted this way. The clique is a monster bully, and you should try not to hurt yourself because of their stupidity."

The choice Marissa was forced to make helped her to learn her potential. This is important for young females. Most girls want to be able to voice their opinions openly and feel assertive rather than passive. They want to be the doers, not the ones who watch what is being done.

Young teens are very often thought of as troublemakers by parents, teachers, and other adults. This label is most often unfair. Girls are often just reaching for recognition and to have their actions acknowledged. Girls who have trouble at school often go unnoticed, as they are quiet sufferers. Teachers consider them to be overwhelmed but getting along with the work. The behavior of boys who need help at school is often much different. They stand out, assert themselves, and make waves. Girls just try to grin and bear it and mask their pain and shame.

The social scene is often more important to girls than to boys. Girls can sometimes have a problem because of the importance they place on a social issue or problem. A boy does not usually take issues to heart as a girl does. They both care about social issues and conditions, but girls usually will take that caring a step further.

Finding a satisfying activity or developing a talent are choices that can raise self-esteem.

How Can Schools Make Life Easier?

Students between the ages of ten and fifteen can be hard for teachers to reach. Educators and psychologists who study this age group recommend smaller classes, teachers who move along with the kids to the next grade, and providing mentors and role models for girls. Also, using subject matter designed to meet the social and emotional needs of this special age as well as the academic needs is important.

Paula Gardiner and other school counselors explain that cliques exist solely for power. Sadly, it is power that is used to hurt and manipulate people. The girls in a clique become the dictators of the school or a portion of it. The power of the clique comes from subtle use of manipulation (making someone do something). Cliques also rule social events such as parties, and often girls are hurt by being left out. Cliques appeal to young people at a time when they are starting to separate from the family. Cliques do not appear every once in a while. They happen like clockwork year after year. Each year a new clique may surface, but it unfortunately is just like those before it.

SITUATION
You are in an Internet chat room and the conversation seems strange or scary.

GOOD CHOICE
Leave the chat room. Report the problem to your online server or the police.

Members of an clique help establish its exclusivity and its designated territory. The members of the clique become skilled at using social blackmail to get what they want. You can sit at their table *if* you give up your other best friends or a boyfriend whom the girls do not like. No member of a clique is interested in loyalty, honesty, affection, or feelings for other people. Those human traits are not considered "cool" by a clique. If you start showing these traits, you are pushed out. If the clique members see you talking with a boy whom they feel should date one of them, you are out. If you take a ride in an "uncool" boy's car, you are out. Behavior must be that which is established as "cool" by the clique. Cliques exploit the human desire of young girls to be with friends.

Help from a School Counselor

If cliques happen year after year, what can a girl do to avoid getting tangled up in this trauma? Every girl will handle this her own way, but answering these questions may help you protect yourself.

1. What do you want to get out of this friendship?
2. Do you have things in common with the clique?
3. What is the purpose of the group?
4. Do you fear doing something that will make them kick you out of the clique?
5. What other choices do you have?

Answering these five questions should help you to see that this is not a group with democratic ideals and that friendship means nothing to them. Only power is craved at all costs.

Gardiner also has some ideas for using your time while breaking out of a clique. "Learn to keep a journal where you can write your good experiences. Write letters to a distant friend or cousin to get a fresh view of being a young teen. Write poems, cook desserts, grow herbs, train the dog, meet kids from a nearby

Real friends care about each other's feelings.

school who want to stay away from cliques, read some books, sign up to tutor kids, go to the movies, or rent a tape. Just do things that make you happy and help you feel good."

Never think that losing the clique is the worst thing that can ever happen to you. In a few years you will see that it was actually a gift—a gift of freedom, individualism, and ease. Remember what happened to Marissa? She used soccer to take up the space left by the clique. She also tried art and music classes to bring out her creative talents. Her art became quite good, and she pursued it, earning a scholarship to an art school. She knows her decision to leave that toxic clique was the best thing she ever did. If she had toughed it out and eventually been accepted back in, she would have sacrificed her personal development. Her art talent would have been undiscovered. Do not let a clique damage your gentle side or your friendships.

Passing Gently Through Grief

9

SPRING

The ice on the pond
Will someday melt
Away.
After the storm
Of pain cold
A time of mourning
For those lost
Leaving the water
Clear and refreshing
The blackness of death
Like the cold ice.
Yet
Leaves room
For life to grow
Anew

Every painful loss causes grief.

THUY (SOUNDS LIKE TWEE) had been in America for ten years when her world stopped short. As a chubby, happy four-year-old, Thuy came from her homeland in Vietnam to live in San Francisco, California. Her father, a photographer, found work with a weekly newspaper. Thuy's mother worked in a nail salon as soon as her English could be understood by the customers. Thuy stayed with a neighbor until she started kindergarten. English was still hard for her, but she worked and studied, and neighbors helped her with spelling and math. By seventh grade she was proud of her progress. She had four best friends and kind, if somewhat old-fashioned, parents.

Each day, Thuy took the bus to school and waited for her favorite class. The school's art studio was wonderful! Thuy could disappear into colors and pictures of her old country. The teacher, Ms. Lindel, encouraged Thuy and even told her she was a very promising artist. Thuy visited Ms. Lindel's class whenever she could. They talked about famous artists and how Thuy might be able to go to art school during the summer. As the school year progressed, Ms. Lindel said she had found a terrific art school for her, and a scholarship was offered for girls ages twelve to sixteen if a teacher recommended the student.

Thuy took the papers to show her parents and other relatives. By now, her brother, two aunts, a grandmother, and a cousin had also left Vietnam, and they all lived near her family. It was a big, noisy group, and Thuy loved all the visiting and fun and food. That afternoon, she ran up into her house expecting her mother to be there, as she didn't work on Wednesdays. The house was dark and empty. They got a snack and sat down to read the scholarship papers. After a couple of hours, Thuy thought it was strange that neither parent had called to see if she was home safe and starting her homework.

Another thirty minutes passed and Thuy's aunt came into the house. Her usually bright face was masked by a deep sadness, and Thuy's stomach began to feel as if she were bouncing up and down on a trampoline. Her aunt took Thuy's hands and kissed her cheek. "Come sit on the sofa with me," she said. Looking into Thuy's frightened eyes, the aunt told Thuy that "there had been a bad accident." Thuy's father had dropped off her mother for a dentist appointment and then they met for a late lunch. On the way home, a drunk driver had crossed the street divider and flipped his car, landing on Thuy's parents' car. They were trapped and crushed by the other driver's heavier car. The police and paramedics were called and came quickly, but it was too late. There was no way to save them.

Thuy's aunt begged her to come home with her. "Be with me in my little house and we can mourn together. The rest of the family will gather there as they are told of the accident." Thuy simply stared at her aunt. It was too hard to take in all of this. Her parents had been killed in the middle of a warm, sunny day by a drunk. Thuy walked up the stairs as if in a trance and packed a small bag to take to her aunt's house. So many questions and feelings filled her brain, and she held her head tight as if to keep it from falling off her shoulders.

Two weeks later, Thuy was still with her aunt and had not gone back to school. She didn't speak to anyone.

What Do the Experts Say?

Thuy's aunt took her to a grief therapist, Dr. Minette Amir, a woman who works with people who have suffered great losses. Thuy still would not speak. The therapist told Thuy's aunt "that even children need to grieve. Without grieving and then releasing the grief and pain, Thuy would go on being sick." On the way home, they passed Ms. Lindel. Thuy called her name and Ms. Lindel came to the car, opened the door, and took Thuy into her arms. Thuy hugged Ms. Lindel for what seemed like hours but was really just ten minutes. When Thuy asked if she could still go to summer art school, Ms. Lindel smiled and said, "Yes, it was all arranged."

Thuy lived with her aunt until she graduated from high school and left to go to art college. Her family was very proud of her. She still thought about her parents and kept their picture on her dresser. Every day that passed helped her to end her grieving and then rebuild her life. She volunteered for Students Against Drunk Drivers and slowly worked through all her feelings by helping to prevent others from experiencing such loss. Thuy continued to work with her grief therapist throughout high school and college.

Grief, as the therapist pointed out, is an emotion. Almost everyone experiences it at some time. Grief is an emotional response to a painful loss. Grief may start as early as when an individual first learns that there will be a future loss. Some examples of situations that can cause a grief reaction might include being told you must move to another state and miss the prom, learning that a pet is dying, or being told by friends that

they do not want to be with you any more. The grieving can also come on news of loss. Dr. Amir adds that "this process of grieving is normal, and it allows a person to slowly accept changes that are beyond her control."

Religious Leaders Also Help People Through Grief

Most ethnic and religious groups have traditions for helping people through the grieving period. These traditions have developed through the centuries. They bring comfort to those who grieve and allow friends and family to be with the person who has suffered the loss.

Reverend Linda Stephens comments, "These practices are designed primarily to meet the needs of adults. Often adolescent girls are overwhelmed by the loss and then all the activity that surrounds it. There are no separate practices for young teens, and this leaves many girls without a healthy outlet for their grief." Like Thuy, many girls stop talking or close off all feeling in an effort to stop that one giant hurt.

"Many times, adolescents may not recognize an event as a loss and may feel the pain alone, not knowing how to handle it. Girls often do not realize that the grieving is a natural, necessary response to an emotional loss. These examples of loss may help girls and their parents recognize grief reactions and thus understand a young teen's behavior," explains Stephens:

- A sudden death of a loved one
- Loss of a parent through divorce
- Discovering a chronic illness
- Losing a body part in an accident
- Receiving a serious medical report
- The death of a pet or a friend
- Moving away from the family house
- Destruction of a home in a fire or other catastrophe

Violence at schools causes emotional pain for the whole community.

- Failing once again, after putting forth a best effort
- Missing a holiday due to an illness
- Having to give up a cherished dream

Suffering a significant loss, even if it seems important only to you, causes grief. Time and rebuilding a sense of "balance" or normalcy in your life is needed before you can stop grieving. The actions of grief-stricken people vary. Reverend Stephens notes, "To some degree, your cultural and religious beliefs play a part in how you will grieve. Your personality is also a large part of the way you choose to grieve. Mourning is just one part of the whole grieving response. Anger at the loss, pain from the suddenness and emptiness a loss leaves, a search for an answer to why, and a desire to wipe it all away and start over are also part of the overall grieving process."

Stephens says it is important to understand that what you think or feel is grief. She explains, "There are actual stages to grieving, and they usually occur in a particular sequence. If you do not grieve in this order or experience every stage, do not be concerned. Some individuals do not go from stage to stage, or follow this order. Some experience two or three stages at the same time. There is no limit on how long you stay in a stage, and no rule that you must do each one."

Generally speaking, the stages of grief are:

- Denial. Shock or disbelief are the two most common denial emotions; however, you may also feel a rejection of reality and even physical reactions such as faintness, nausea, confusion, and claustrophobia—a fear of being closed in.

- Anger. You feel impatient, unable to cooperate, bitter, helpless, and sarcastic.
- Bargaining. Exhausted or depressed, you make final attempts to avoid the reality of your loss. You may feel weak and depleted by your efforts. You may try to get a loved one back by saying, "If I am good, Mom will return" or "If I get my grades up, Mom will still love me."
- Depression. Withdrawing from family, friends, and your normal routine characterize this stage.
- Acceptance. This final stage of grieving is characterized by being contemplative, feeling a return to normalcy, and having the ability to talk about the loss without bouncing back into one of the previous stages.

As grief is hard to recognize, how can a young teen know that's what she is suffering from and not something else? If a person is unable to grieve, it may be because of an unresolved issue with the person who has died. Sometimes people throw themselves into work or act strangely by drinking or overeating. "If you feel like this, then you aren't dealing with the grief, but instead you are trying to smother it out of your life. If you are experiencing the steps explained above, then you are grieving. It is a normal emotion and reaction to loss," explains Stephens.

Occasionally people view grieving as a sign of weakness. More often someone will hold back the grieving experience so as to be strong for the rest of the family. But the person who is the "strong" one only grieves more as everyone else reaches the stage of acceptance. The strong one has held the family together and now must begin to grieve just as the others finish.

How you grieve is actually a choice that you make. That choice is influenced by the extent of the loss in your life, your personality, your religious beliefs, and your cultural background. Some people are taught not to cry, even when grieving. How you show your grief and when is your choice. There is no absolutely wrong or right way to grieve, but going through the process is necessary if you want to get back to your life.

When people find it impossible to let out the pain, or they experience great shock, going to a mental health professional is

At group sessions, a grief counselor works with teens.

very important. A person trained to help those who need to grieve can advise you and your family and help to sort out feelings. If you want to make a choice that is based on information, always talk to your therapist or counselor. Your school or public library and bookstores have self-help books designed to encourage your understanding of the grieving process. There may be suggestions in the back of the book for websites, counseling, self-help groups, or support groups. The choice of how to work through your grief may not seem obvious to you at first. If you let yourself feel emotions and open up to the feelings of your family, it is easier to begin grieving.

Rabbi Joseph Berger explains, "As with many other emotions, even grieving needs to slowly come to an end. This doesn't mean you have to forget the person or how much they meant to you. Instead, as your grief gets under control, you choose how to keep a memory of the person. Many people choose to visit the grave and place flowers or other evidence of their visit. In some religions, it is customary to have the whole family visit the grave eleven months after the death so that the family members do not grieve for a whole year. Some people cover the mirrors in every room. Others do not believe in a wife remarrying. Many religions send flowers and others believe in cremation [burning the body and coffin]. These traditions are based on many years of going through grief and finding sources of relief or aid. Then after many years these actions become the tradition in a family, religion, or culture."

For Thuy, the grieving process was very difficult and long. Finally, with her art teacher's help and with the help of a grief therapist, Thuy was able to visit her parent's graves and cry. Now Thuy and her aunt go every month to put flowers on their graves and to tell her parents about their lives.

The grieving process is a natural and normal way to deal with a person's death. If you find yourself having difficulty organizing your thoughts, have negative views on everything, feel a sense of guilt or worthlessness, or have feelings of hopelessness, get help, as these are not part of the grieving process. If you are depressed about the loss or death of a person and think about dying yourself, it is important for you to seek out a therapist.

If following traditional grieving steps becomes too difficult or too sad and lonely for you, ask a family adult to help you. Your request will help the adult through his or her grief as well.

Many young teens find that making their own special reminder of the person and then putting that on the grave is a way to end the grieving. Others make peace with feelings by going to the grave to say good-bye and release any anger that might still linger.

Linda Goldman, a grief therapist in the Maryland Center for Loss and Grief Therapy, feels it is extremely important for girls to know that grief changes as a female goes through different stages of her life. "Grief changes developmentally; for example, at seven years of age, a child is distraught over the loss of a parent and feels that loss daily as the nurturing person who did things for her is gone. If the surviving parent remarries, a young girl grieves again as she fears that the parent is now lost. As a teenager, a female often regrieves over the loss of her mom or dad, who is not there to help with the daughter's new body changes and teenage feelings. As each important life event occurs, the girl regrieves the loss of her parent who is not there to see a graduation, a scholarship, college experiences, first loves, marriage, and the birth of her own children. Girls also fear that the surviving parent might start to date, which would make it feel as if that parent is leaving too. As the living parent and other family members understand that periods of grief will continue to attack this young woman, we need to be there to help her."

Choices are many. How you choose to carry on your grieving stages and how you end it are up to you. Only you know how you feel and what will allow you to feel better.

A Last Note About this Book

Each chapter of this book has offered information for you to use to make choices. Some of these choices are harder than others,

With time to grieve and considerate friends, teens can come through a loss to regain a sense of joy.

and some may be new to you. It is important to recognize that there are always choices and to try to make the most informed choice. Making choices and decisions is an adult skill that everyone needs to begin practicing early in life so as to be good at responsibility as an adult. Good decisions are necessary for succeeding at jobs, selecting friends, planning your future, studying at school, and being safe.

Dear Parents and Caregivers

TOOTH FAIRY

Ever since I was a pea in size
All I ever heard was lies.
What no Easter Bunny or Santa Claus?
Don't play with dolls.

It won't hurt. It'll grow back.
In the meantime wear a hat.
Remember when you were seven?
Rusty went to doggie heaven.

Love makes babies. A kiss can heal.
Kids in China don't eat meals.
You can be anything you want to be.

A doctor, a dancer, a chimpanzee.
Bedbugs bite. The Bogeyman's there.
A quarter for a tooth.

I wish everyone would grow up
And tell the truth.
Medicine does taste bad and
Superman is not your dad.

Dear parents and caregivers:

In all my years of writing for children and teens, this is my first letter to the caregivers of my readers. To encourage your daughter's ability to become a decision maker I hope you will read any parts of this book that she may request. Your own value system also needs to be added in this book. An important theme throughout the book is that girls have choices and need to learn to make good ones. Several adolescents read the manuscript as it developed, and the individual chapters developed from their thoughts, questions, and concerns. I know there are likely to be additional issues not covered by this book but that are of importance to you.

Parents of teenagers often say that their daughter used to be so easy, so willing to follow rules and accept a share of responsibility. Yet, as ages ten, eleven, and twelve came along, that sweet child turned into a nightmare adolescent. In working with parents and their daughters, I've observed that not only the child changes. For individual reasons, with safety and good intentions on their minds, parents also change. As there is no operating manual for raising girls, it is important to keep certain ideas in your mind so that you use them as much as possible. These suggestions can help you turn a potential nightmare into a sweet dream.

1. How you say something to an adolescent is as important as what you say. Avoid guilt and blame by saying, "I feel angry" rather than "You make me angry." The choice to be angry is yours and is not the fault of your daughter, although what she has done might have triggered it. Do not make her feel that she is the cause.

Spending family time together, being generous with praise and affection, can accomplish more than discipline and rules.

2. Underdiscipline rather than overdiscipline. Adolescents feel useless when we ask them to be responsible but do not give them a chance to show that they can be. Also, mistakes will happen. Give a second and third chance, but be sure the consequences of lying or disregarding rules are made clear in advance.

3. We spend many hours hugging our infants and toddlers, but can you count the number of hugs or kisses exchanged with your daughter in the last three days? We tend to think that they are too old for displays of affection. They may even push us aside. But the reality is that young girls are starved for those hugs that tell them they are worthwhile and loved. Do it often enough, and you may need fewer rules and less discipline.

4. Self-esteem is vital for all people, but especially for young female teens. Being trusted teaches trustworthiness. Being overtly loved teaches them how to love. They are not so grown-up that a good role model isn't important. Be the kind of person you want your daughter to be as a teen and as an adult. Allow her to learn affection, self-esteem, sense of worth, and how to love from you.

5. Dwell on your messages of encouragement and faith rather than on her mistakes. Try not to point out shortcomings and speak in sarcastic tones. These become arrows to her heart (and maybe tattoos on her thigh)!

6. Your voice and mannerisms carry a message. Shaking your head from side to side while questioning "what will become of this child" will make her ask the same question of herself. She needs those answers from you. Do not ridicule. It isn't funny.

7. The words you use also send hidden messages. "Let me do that for you" translates to her as "You are incompetent." "Don't bother me when I am watching my favorite show" translates to "You are unimportant."

8. Similarly, saying you are interested in her but continuing to type your e-mail says "I'm not really interested in you."

Your child's adolescence is often the strangest period of parent-hood. Your daughter is sensitive yet plays football with the boys. She wants to go to the movies with you but brings two friends and sits with them. Trying to understand her way of thinking can be very confusing, but it is definitely not the time to give up. Remember, she'll soon get a job, drive a car, and be making all of her own decisions.

Thanks for reading,
Judith Greenberg

CHAMPION

When you can't go
Anymore,
Not one step more,
And you are tired,
No you are exhausted,
You go that last mile
That one last lap.
Because somewhere
Inside you
There is a champion.
And when you are pushed
To the limit,
You can go no farther.
The champion
That is you
Comes out and
Goes that last mile
That last step.

Alcohol–Drug Use Questionnaire

Divide a sheet of paper into two columns, one marked "YES" and the other marked "NO." Read each statement carefully. If the statement says something true about you, put a check under YES. If it says something that is not true about you, put a check under NO. Some of these questions apply to teens and adults; others only to adults. YES answers are signals of alcohol or drug use problems.

1. Do you feel that your alcohol/drug use is not normal?
2. Did you ever wake up in the morning after drinking or drug use the night before and find that you could not remember part of that evening?
3. Do your parents worry or complain about your drinking or drug use?
4. Can you not stop drinking or drug use without a struggle?
5. Do you ever feel bad about your drinking or drug use?
6. Do friends or relatives think you are not a normal drinker?
7. Do you ever try to limit your alcohol or drug use to a certain time of day, or to certain places?

8. Are you sometimes unable to stop drinking or drug use even though you want to?

9. Have you ever attended a meeting of Alcoholics Anonymous, Alateen, or Narcotics Anonymous?

10. Have you gotten into fights when using alcohol or drugs?

11. Has drinking or drug use created problems with you and your parents?

12. Has a parent or family member ever needed help with drinking or drug use?

13. Have you lost friends because of your drinking or drug use?

14. Have you gotten into trouble at school or work because of drinking or drug use?

15. Have you ever neglected your schoolwork or other obligations due to drinking or drug use?

16. Have you ever lost a job because of drinking or drug use?

17. Do you drink or use drugs before noon?

18. Has your doctor warned you about your drug or alcohol use?

19. Have you ever had severe shaking, heard voices, or seen things that were not there after heavy drinking or drug use?

20. Have you gone to anyone for help about your drinking or drug use?

21. Have you ever been in a hospital because of drinking or drug use?

22. Have you ever been a patient in a psychiatric hospital or in a psychiatric ward, with drinking or drug use part of the problem?

23. Have you ever been treated at a psychiatric or mental health clinic, or seen a doctor, social worker, or other counselor for

help with an emotional problem in which drinking or drug use played a part?

24. Have you ever been arrested or stopped for drunk driving, or driving after drinking? If yes, how many times?

25. Have you ever been arrested, or held, because of drunk behavior? If yes, how many times?

26. Have you ever been arrested, or held, because of involvement with drugs? If yes, how many times?

To Find Out More

Books

An anonymous teenager. *It Happened to Nancy*. New York: Beatrice Sparks/Avon Books, 1994.

Angelou, Maya. *The Heart of a Woman*. New York: Bantam Books, 1981.

Angelou, Maya. *I Know Why the Caged Bird Sings*. New York: Bantam Books, 1993.

Arnothy, Christine. *I Am Fifteen—and I Don't Want to Die*. New York: Scholastic, 1956.

Bell, Ruth. *Changing Bodies, Changing Lives: A Book for Teens on Sex and Relationships*. New York: Vintage Books, 1987.

Berry, Carmen Renee, and Tamara Traeder. *Girlfriends: Invisible Bonds, Enduring Ties*. Berkeley, California: Wild Cat Press, 1995.

Bode, Janet. *Kids Still Having Kids*. Rev. ed. Danbury, Connecticut: Franklin Watts, 1999.

Carlip, Hillary. *Girl Power: Young Women Speak Out*. New York: Warner Books, 1995.

Dee, Catherine. *The Girl's Guide to Life: How to Take Charge of the Issues That Affect You.* New York: Little Brown, 1997.

EDK Associates. *Teenagers Under Pressure.* New York: *Seventeen* and the Ms. Foundation for Women, 1996.

Ford, Michael Thomas. *The Voices of AIDS.* New York: Beech Tree, 1995.

Goldman, Jane. *A Teenager's Safety Guide: Street Smarts.* New York: Barron's, 1995.

Isler, Charlotte, and Alwyn T. Cohall, M.D. *The Watts Teen Health Dictionary.* Danbury, Connecticut: Franklin Watts, 1996.

Johnston, Andrea. *Girls Speak Out: Finding Your True Self.* New York: Scholastic Press, 1997.

Maynard, R.A. *Kids Having Kids: A Robin Hood Foundation Special Report on the Costs of Adolescent Child Bearing.* New York: Robin Hood Foundation,1996.

Ojeda, Linda. *Safe Dieting for Teens.* Alameda, California: Hunter House Inc. Publishers, 1993.

Pennock, Michael Francis. *What We Really Want to Know: 101 Questions That Teens Always Ask.* Indiana: Ave Maria Pratt, 1996.

Pipher, Mary. *Reviving Ophelia: Saving the Selves of Adolescent Girls.* New York: *Alantime,* March 1994.

Sanders, Bill. *Straight Talk for Girls.* Michigan: Fleming H. Revell, 1995.

Terkel, Susan. *Finding Your Way: A Book about Sexual Ethics.* Danbury, Connecticut: Franklin Watts, 1995.

Online Sites

Adolescence Directory On-line is a website offering information on adolescent issues.

http://education.indiana.edu/cas/adol/adol.html

Campaign for Our Children offers news, advice, and information for teens.

www.cfoc.org/3_teen/3-index.cfm

How to Talk to Your Child About Sexuality: Planned Parenthood, 1-800-230-PLAN, or

www.plannedparenthood.com

Mothers Against Drunk Driving (MADD):

www.madd.org

National Campaign to Prevent Teen Pregnancy provides statistics, information, and resources.

www.teenpregnancy.org/index.html

Rape, Abuse, and Incest National Network:

www.rainn.org

Student Leadership Services website focuses on student leadership and substance abuse.

www.sadd.org

Suicide Prevention Advocacy Network: *www.spanusa.org*

Welcome to the 12-Step Cyber Cafe (substance abuse):

www.12steps.org

Toll-Free Hotlines

The toll-free phone numbers listed below offer help in a crisis. Numbers with (TDD) beside them are for hearing-impaired callers.

AIDS Hotline
800-590-2437

AIDS Hotline for Hearing Impaired
800-243-7889 (TDD)

AIDS Hotline in Spanish
800-344-SIDA (7432)

Battered Women's Justice Project
800-903-0111, ext. 3
A resource advocacy center providing assistance with defense teams for battered women charged with crimes.

Boys Town Suicide and Community Crisis Line
800-448-3000, 800-448-1833 (TDD)
Referrals to local resources: suicide, pregnancy, runaways and abuse.

CDC National AIDS Hotline
800-342-AIDS (2437)
Referrals to local hotlines, testing centers, counseling, and information.

CDC National STD Hotline
800-227-8922
Referrals to public clinics, prevention, symptoms, treatment.

Child Find of America Hotline

800-I-AM-LOST (426-5678)

Looks for missing and abducted children.

Childhelp U.S. National Child Abuse Hotline

800-4-A-CHILD (422-4453), 800-2-A CHILD (TDD)

Provides multilingual counseling on child abuse.

Covenant House Hotline

800-999-9999

Referrals throughout the United States. A resource for drug abuse, homelessness, and runaways.

Domestic Violence/Child Abuse/Sexual Abuse

National Domestic Violence Hotline

800-799-SAFE (7233), 800-787-3224 (TDD)

Referrals to local services and shelters for victims of partner or spousal abuse.

Equal Rights Advocates

800-839-4372

Sexual harassment.

Mexican American Legal Defense and Education Fund

213-629-2512

Class action litigation.

National Child Safety Council Childwatch

800-222-1464

Answers and literature on safety, drug abuse, and household dangers.

National Cocaine Hotline

800-COCAINE (262-2363)

Rehabilitation centers for all types of drug dependency.

National Domestic Violence Hotline

800-799-SAFE (7233)

Crisis assistance, information about shelters, legal advocacy, health care centers, and counseling.

National Drug Information Treatment and Referral Hotline

800-662-HELP (4357)

Rehabilitation center for drug or alcohol problems.

National Gay and Lesbian Hotline

800-347-TEEN (8336)

A telephone resource for gay, lesbian, transgendered and questioning young people up to age twenty-four.

National Hotline for Missing and Exploited Children

800-843-5678

A hotline for reporting and sighting missing children.

National Runaway Switchboard

800-621-4000

Crisis intervention and travel assistance for runaways.

National Victim Center

800-FYI-CALL

Counseling and referrals for victims.

National Youth Crisis Hotline

800-422-HOPE (4673)

Referrals to local drug treatment centers, shelters, and counseling. Resources: pregnancy, suicide, molestation, child abuse.

RAINN Hotline

800-656-HOPE

A last resort for rape, abuse, or incest victims.

Index

144